Dining Services Cleaning & Sanitation Procedures

Enhancing Employee Cleaning, Foodhandling & Sanitation Skills

Digna I Cassens, MHA, RDN, CLT, FAND

First Edition, October 2018
Copyright DNMS2018
    Digna I Cassens, MHA, RDN, CLT, FAND

This book is written to provide detailed cleaning procedures and instructions for dining services departments for physical plant and equipment in institutional kitchens. The instructions are appropriate for all size kitchens in long-term care communities, residential, assisted living and congregate living centers ranging in bed sizes from 30 to 500. It is intended as a reference only and not to replace procedures or training or the training provided by your employer. The guidelines are and in compliance with standards of practice in healthcare facilities and are consistent with regulatory requirements and standards.

This book is protected by copyright. No part of this book may be reproduced or transmitted in any form or by any means, including as photocopies or scanned-in or other electronic copies, or utilized by any information storage and retrieval system without written permission from the publishers. To request permission please submit a written request to Cassens Associates – Diversified Nutrition Management Systems.

Published by:
    Cassens Associates – Diversified Nutrition Management Systems
    558 Tahoe Avenue
    Yucca Valley, CA 92284
    cassensdigna@gmail.com

ISBN-10:   0-9981430-2-6
ISBN-13:   978-0-9981430-2-6

Printed and manufactured in the United States of America
First Printing: 2018 Cassens Associates

PREFACE

This book is a compilation of some of my lifetime work in long-term care communities and as an educator. I believe that knowledge is power, and the happiest staff is well trained staff. I have a lifetime teaching credential with the California Community Colleges qualifying me to teach basic culinary, foodservice and nutrition classes and conducted credentialing classes for dietary managers.

My consulting experience in long-term care facilities developing policies and procedures and training programs for foodservice and nursing staff in long-term-care made me realize how limited and valuable time is in this industry. Busy schedules are spent providing direct consulting services and do not not allow much time program and procedures development. I often wished I had a resource with ready to use cleaning procedures I could use instead. This publication is a convenient tool box to either base your own procedures on, or to use as written as your own cleaning procedures manual.

For additional training information and procedures I recommend you also purchase the Dining Services Education & Dining Services Training and Orientation for Cooks.

If you you find this book useful in your practice please look for my other books.

http://www.nutritionmanagementsystems.org
http://www.flavorfulfortifiedfood.com

DEDICATION

    This book would not be a reality without the staff I have worked with. I've had the good fortune of working with outstanding registered dietitian nutritionists, dietetic technicians registered, dietary managers, cooks and dining services aides. They've inspired and encouraged me throughout my career and taught me time saving methods I didn't know about.

Digna Irizarry Cassens

About Me

Digna Cassens, MHA, RDN, CLT, FAND

I'm a registered dietitian nutritionist (RDN), owner of a micro-practice, Diversified Nutrition Management System. I have a BS in Foods & Nutrition and completed a dietetic internship, a Masters degree in Healthcare Administration and have lifetime teaching credentials for Community Colleges in California. As a Certified LEAP Therapist I treat clients with food sensitivities as well as chronic diseases, weight issues and allergies. I'm very active in the Academy of Nutrition and Dietetics (AND) and belong to several practice groups contributing as a volunteer member of various committees. During my long-years in the profession I've received many honors, such as the 2014 Distinguished Member Award from Dietetics in Healthcare Communities (DHCC) and the 2015 Excellence in Communication, Consulting and Private Practice Award from the California Academy of Nutrition and Dietetics.

I launched my company in 2011 after many decades in the corporate world. I now limit my practice to consulting for homes for adults with intellectual and physical disabilities and assisted living centers. I also continue to provide nutrition and wellness counseling to individuals and groups and occasionally accept speaking engagements. Currently I live in the Mohave Desert area in Southern California and spend my time developing healthy, nutritious recipes, writing, tending to my rescued animals and amphibians, and indulging in my hobbie, genealogy

My publications include *Flavorful Fortified Food – Recipes to Enrich your Life, Food First - Enhancing the Quality of Life using Fortified Food, Food for Group Homes, Simplified Diets and Nutrition Guidelines, Spice it Up With Robust Flavor – Delicious Recipes for Wellness, Dining Services Orientation and Training for Cooks and Dining Services Education & Training Manual.*

Connect with me and get to know me better.

http://www.facebook.com/cassensassociates,
http://www.nutritionmanagementsystems.org, https://twitter.com/@digtheisland,
https://www.pinterest.com/digtheisland, instagram.com/digtheisland,
https://www.linkedin.com/in/digna-cassens-mha-rdn-clt

Although we take it for granted, sanitation is a physical measure that has probably done more to increase human life span than any kind of drug or surgery

Deepak Chopra

INDEX
by page & procedure number

PROCEDURE NUMER	TOPIC	PAGE
i	Title page	*I*
ii	Copyrights & Credits	*ii*
iii	Preface	*iii*
iv	Dedication	*iv*
v	About Me	*v*
vi	Deepak Chopra – Sanitation Quote	*vi*
vii	Table of Contents - Procedures and Sections	*vii*
A	Sanitation Standards	*1*
A1	Employee Health and Personal Hygiene	*3*
A2	Empolyee Health and Safety	*4*
A3	Food Sanitation & Safety Guidelines	*5*
A4	Safety and Accident Prevention Management	*9*
B	Cleaning and Sanitation Procedures	*12*
B1	Food Thermometer Calibration	*13*
B2	Cleaning of Dining Areas	*14*
B3	Cleaning of Can Opener and Base	*15*
B4	Walls and Ceilings	*16*
B5	Shelves, Contertops and Other Surfaces	*17*
B6	Cleaning of Floors	*19*
B7	Cleaning of Coffee Brewing Equipment	*20*
B8	Monitoring Dishwashing Machines	*22*
B9	General Dishroom Sanitation	*26*

INDEX
by page & procedure number

PROCEDURE NUMER	TOPIC	PAGE
B10	Machine Dishwashig, Drying and Storage	27
B11	Manual Dishwashing	29
B12	Dispensing Equipment	31
B12	Juice Dispenser	31
B12	Milk Dispenser	31
B13	Dry Storage Areas	33
B14	Electrical Food Machines	35
B15	Prevention of Rodent Infestaton	37
B16	Hoods, Vents and Filters	38
B17	Hot Food Tables, Tray Carts, Shelves	39
B18	Cleaning of Ice Machines	41
B18	Ice Maker Manufacturer Instructions page	42
B18	Cleaning and Storage of Ice Scoop	42
B19	Ingredients Bins	43
B20	Storage of Cleaning Supplies and Janitor's Closet	44
B21	Handling of Mops and Buckets	45
B22	Pest Control and Monitoring	46
B23	Cleaning of Ranges and Ovens	47
B24	Cleaning of Refrigerators and Freezers – Dietary	48
B25	Cleaning of Refrigerators in Resident Rooms	50
B26	Sanitizing Cloths in Red Sanitizing Buckets	51
B26	Green Buckets	52
B27	Cleaning of Steamers and Steam Kettles	53

INDEX
by page & procedure number

PROCEDURE NUMER	TOPIC	PAGE
B28	Cleaning of Refrigerators in Nursing Units & Pantries	54
B28	Patient Refrigerators Outside of Kitchen	54
C	Forms Records and Logs	55
C1	Sanitation Review With comments	56
C2	Food Temperature Cooling Log	59
C3	Cleaning Schedule Assignments & Procedures	60
C4	Temperature Recods 　　Cooking Temperature Record	62
C5	Deliveries Temperature Record	63
C6	Freezer Temperature Record	64
C7	Refrigerator Temperature Record	65
C8	Cooking and Cooling Log	66
C9	Pots and Pans Sanitizer/Temperature Log	67
C10	Thermometer Calibration Record	68
C11	Storage Log – Refrigerator – Freezer	69
C12	Cleaning Schedule Assignments & Procedure	70
C13	Pre-Meal Checklist	73
C14	Daily Kitchen Cleaning Schedule	74
C15	Weekly Kitchen Cleaning Schedule – Jan To June	75
C16	Weekly Kitchen Cleaning Schedule – June to Dec	76
C17	Monthly Kitchen Cleaning Schedule	77
C18	Production Schedules and Standards 　　HACCP Based Instructions	78
C19	Hazard Analysis Table – Process Step	80
C20	HACCP Plan Summary –ROP CCP HACCP	81

INDEX
by page & procedure number

PROCEDURE NUMER	TOPIC	PAGE
C21	Storage Time and Temperature Guidelines	82
C22	Quality Assessment of a Meal	83
C23	Pest Control Monitoring Record	84
D	Food Sanitation & Safety – Purpose	85
D1	Food From Outside Sources	86
D2	HACCP Management	88
D3	Temperature Guidelines	92
D4	Safe Use of Gloves	93
D5	Common Causes of Foodborne Illness Food Safety Regulations	96
D6	Food Temperature Safety	99
D6	MinimuM Safe Internal Cooking Temperatures	100
D6	Food Safety Tips	101
E	Competence	103
E1	Working Healthy Quiz Questions and Answers	104
E2	Working Safely Quiz Questions and Answers	108
E4	Competence Assessment (Observation)	111
F	Resources and References	112
G	Index & Table of Contents - Alphabetical	114

SANITATION STANDARDS   A

The Dietary Manager (DM) is responsible for maintaining standards of sanitation and, under the supervision of the Administrator, for maintenance and repair of kitchen facilities and repair. Sanitary conditions will be maintained in the storage, preparation and distribution areas of food in compliance with quality assurance standards and federal and local regulations.

1. A specific cleaning schedule is maintained, indicating items to be cleaned, frequency and position responsible.

2. The schedule is posted in the Dietary Services Department and monitored by the Dietary Manager (DM)

3. Procedures for cleaning all equipment and work areas are available and followed consistently

4. Dishwashing procedures and techniques are carried out in compliance with State and local codes.

5. Written reports of inspections by State and/or local health authorities are kept on file with notations made of action taken to comply with plan of correction.

6. Waste not disposed of by mechanical means is to be double-bagged and kept in leak-proof non-absorbent containers, with close-fitting covers, and disposed of daily in a manner that will prevent transmission of disease, a breeding place for flies or a feeding place for rodents. Waste containers are thoroughly cleaned inside and outside each time they are emptied.

7. Dry or staple food items are stored above the floor in a ventilated room, which is not subject to sewage or waste water backflow, or contamination by condensation, leakage, rodents or vermin. Dry storage ambient temperature should not exceed 85°F.

8. Handwashing facilities, including hot and cold water, soap, individual disposable towels and covered garbage container with foot pedal will be provided in the Dietary Services Department.

SANITATION STANDARDS A

9. Procedures for equipment sanitation are kept in each facility's Maintenance and Sanitation section of the Dietary Policy and Procedure Manual. Employees are responsible for attending training and reading the required instructions and procedures.

10. The Registered Dietitian Nutritionist validates general sanitation standards are maintained routinely and assists with correcting any areas of out of compliance.

11. The DM is responsible for implementation and compliance. Administrator monitors for compliance.

EMPLOYEE HEALTH AND PERSONAL HYGIENE   A-1

Food handlers are the single, most-common source of food contamination. By practicing good personal hygiene habits, you can help drastically reduce the cause of illness and incidence of infection in the facility. It is your responsibility to maintain good personal hygiene habits and learn safe food-handling practices. As a dining services food handler, your personal hygiene habits should include the following:

- Using precautions to prevent contamination
- Maintaining good personal health
- Cultivating and maintaining clean personal habits
- Washing your hands frequently

Maintaining good personal hygiene habits is more than just "looking good." It is the responsibility of every dining services department staff member to ensure that any form of personal uncleanliness is replaced with habits that will help prevent illness within the facility and to ensure compliance with facility standards.

The facility ensures that employees' health is protected during working hours, and that employees are competent in personal health and hygiene practices.

1. The Dietary Manager instructs employees on health and personal hygiene.
2. Employees will adhere the facility dress code and wear designated clothing including safe shoes when working in the kitchen.
3. Head covering and restraints are worn to prevent hair falling into food. Approved head coverings include Chef's hats, scarfs or bandanas and hairnets. Sports hats are not included in the approved head covering list and neither are hats or caps from home or worn elsewhere.
4. Nails are short and without polish so they can be kept clean.
5. Jewelry is limited to small earrings, wedding rings, watch and short chains around the neck. Nothing dangling that can fall off or get caught in equipment.
6. Employees will read and understand the Employee Manual and FDA Employee Health and Personal Hygiene Handbook.

Refer to the Empoyee Manual and the FDA
Employee Health and Personal Hygiene Handbook

EMPLOYEE HEALTH AND SAFETY   A-2

HANDWASHING

All dietary employees will use proper handwashing techniques at the designated handwashing sink before starting to work, before and after handling raw food, and after each break to ensure sanitary food and prevent cross-contamination.

PROCEDURE

1. Pull down paper towel.

2. Wash hands well with soap under warm running water, giving particular attention to nails and cuticles.

3. Rinse well.

4. Use paper towel to dry hands and to turn off water.

5. Wash hands before beginning work, after leaving and returning to the kitchen, and in-between performing different tasks.

WHEN TO WASH HANDS

- Before preparing food.
- During food preparation, when switching from raw food to ready-to-eat food.
- During food preparation, as often as needed to remove soil and contamination, and to avoid cross-contaminating food.
- After touching your bare body.
- After using the toilet.
- After touching pets.
- After coughing or sneezing.
- After eating, drinking or using tobacco.
- After anything else that gets your hands dirty.
- Before eating.

FOOD SANITATION & SAFETY GUIDELINES A-3

FOOD STORAGE AND HANDLING

In order to prepare good meals you must start with high quality food which your DSS buys. Correct storage of foods is important.

- Refrigerate foods like meat, poultry, fish, milk, vegetables and fruits as you receive them.

- A refrigerator temperature of below 40°F is needed to keep the food from spoiling.

- Put frozen food in the freezer immediately. Do not refreeze food that has been thawed without first cooking it.

- A freezer temperature of below 0°F is needed to keep frozen food at its best.

- Thawing of meat is allowed only in the refrigerator.

- All meat that may bleed must be thawed and stored on the lower shelves of the refrigerator. Do not store raw meat products near foods to be served raw such as produce, breads, cooked meat and cheese.

- Cover, label, and date all leftover food. Leftover food must be used within 72 hours (3 days). Discard leftover meats in gravy.

- All cooked foods that have to cool must cool down to 70°F within 2 hours, and 40°F within 4 hours.

- Store refrigerated leftover foods in shallow pans so the food will chill quickly. Do not store any food in the same steam table pan it was served in.

- Do not store whole cooked meats (roasts, turkeys). Once cooked, cut into quarters, remove from liquid, and monitor temperatures per temperature log/procedure.

- Rotate canned and dry foods so that older foods are in front or on top of new foods. Use older foods first. Remember the concept "First In First Out" (FIFO).

- Store and label dry bulk foods, like flour and cereal, in covered bins. Labels must include the date opened and the contents (type of food or food name).

- Store scoops in a clean covered container, and not in the bins.

You must have good work habits to protect food from spoiling.

FOOD SANITATION & SAFETY GUIDELINES A-3

Remember these things when you prepare food:

- Handle the food as quickly as possible.

- Handle the food as quickly as possible so that it is not at room temperature for too long. (Food cannot be at room temperature longer than 2 to 4 hours total depending on the type of food) including all preparation and serving time.

- Wash your hands before you start to work.

- Wash hands frequently during the day, and especially before handling food directly with hands.

- Always wash your hands after smoking and using the restroom and then again when going in the kitchen.

- Wear gloves when appropriate, and do not handle anything other than food while wearing gloves.

- Wear clean clothes daily and wear only clothes designated as working clothes or uniforms.

It is much easier to clean your work area as you use it.

Follow these simple rules:

- Wipe up spills when they happen.

- Keep your working counters and the sinks clean.

- Use a germicidal cleaner or sanitizer to wipe cutting boards and counter tops.

- Clean equipment according to the equipment manufacturers' instruction.

FOOD SANITATION & SAFETY GUIDELINES   A-3

<u>Follow these simple rules to keep germs out of food:</u>

- Use tongs, spoons, ladles, scoops or plastic gloves for serving food.

- Put hot food in the pre-heated steamtable just before serving time. (**Not more than 20 minutes.**)

- Keep cold foods such as desserts and beverages, covered and refrigerated until serving time.

- **<u>Do not heat</u>** the steamtable when serving cold plates and salad plates.

- Use ice in the wells to keep cold food cold.

SAFE FOOD TEMPERATURES

The Patients must receive hot food hot and cold food cold. Temperature of regular and puree foods on the stove top, oven or steamtable must be recorded just prior to serving:

- Hot food temperatures must be greater than 160°F.

- Cold food temperatures must be less than 41°F.

- Record food and beverage temperatures either on the menu or a designated form.

FLOOR CARE

FOLLOW THE RIGHT PROCEDURES

The floor must be swept and mopped after each meal or more often, as necessary.

- Clean hot water detergent solution with a germicidal agent must be used. Follow the manufacturer's instructions for how much chemical to use.

- Use "caution" signs on wet floors.

- Mops must be rinsed and hung to air dry after each use.

- Mop heads must be changed daily.

FOOD SANITATION & SAFETY GUIDELINES   A-3

GENERAL CLEANING

FOLLOW THE RIGHT PROCEDURES

The dietary department has a schedule of what equipment must be cleaned, <u>when</u>, <u>how</u>, and by <u>whom</u>.

The safety and sanitation of the food depends on the cleanliness of the dietary department and everyone working in it.

SERVING THE FOOD

To avoid mistakes, check both the diet card and the menu before putting food on the resident's tray. It is important that the resident gets the right food.

<u>Here are some simple rules for serving</u>:

- Check the menu for which specific foods are to be served for each diet.

- Follow all instructions listed on the menus, and the production sheets.

- Food should not run together on the plate; use side dishes for "runny" foods.

- Make use of an attractive garnish such as parsley, apple-ring, etc., on each plate.

- When garnishing Mechanical Soft and Pureed Diets, use garnishes of appropriate texture to prevent choking. Parsley flakes and paprika are appropriate, olives or radishes ARE NOT appropriate.

- Keep clean paper towels on hand to wipe up spills on the edges and bottom of a plate or bowl.

- Wear a cap or hairnet at all times.

- Always wear a clean apron.

SAFETY AND ACCIDENT PREVENTION MANAGEMENT A-4

POLICY

A safe environment will be maintained for residents, staff and visitors.

PROCEDURE

- A. The Dietary Manager (DM) is responsible for accident prevention and the health and safety of the residents relating to the dietary function.
    1. The Dietary Services Department will be represented in the facility Safety Committee.
    2. Dietary employees will participate in the facility's fire, emergency and disaster drills.
    3. Dietary employees will be trained regarding the common causes of accidents, general safety precautions and fire prevention.
    4. In case of employee injuries, reporting procedures are found in RRMf-01 of the Regency Health Services, Inc. Corporate Policy and Procedure Manual. **All injuries must be reported** and the specified procedure followed.

- B. Accident Prevention Guidelines
    1. Good housekeeping and maintaining a clean environment are considered to be one of the most important contributions to a health care facility's accident prevention effort.
    2. Report unsafe conditions or procedures to the Dietary Manager (DM) immediately.
    3. Report all injuries to the Dietary Manager (DM) promptly.
    4. Keep clean. Wash hands thoroughly before handling food or dishes. Wash hands after visiting the restroom and after smoking, to prevent the spread of disease.

- C. Receiving and Storage
    1. Store heavier and bulkier materials on lower shelves.
    2. Use step stools or ladders to reach upper shelves; **never climb on shelves**.
    3. Ask for help when lifting heavy objects.
    4. Follow safe lifting procedures. The Dietary Manager (DM) is responsible for regular and on-going training in safe-lifting procedures.
    5. Use dollies or hand-trucks for transporting materials packaged in heavy bags, crates, boxes, or barrels.
    6. Store cleaning powders, insecticides, and chemicals away from food stuff.

SAFETY AND ACCIDENT PREVENTION MANAGEMENT A-4

D. Floors
1. Keep floors clean, dry, uncluttered, and free of defects that could cause a slip, trip, or fall.
2. Use floor mats in the pot and dishwashing area.
3. Use "*Caution: Wet Floor*" signs to alert all employees.
4. Wear closed-toe shoes with low heels and non-slip soles. Shoes should be leather or vinyl. Cloth shoes are permeable and too soft for protection.

5. During Food Preparation and Service
    1. Use extreme caution with knives:
        a. Cut away from the body.
        b. Keep knives sharp.
        c. Store knives in their proper place, such as knife racks.
        d. Let falling knives fall; do not try to catch them.
        e. Select the appropriate knife for the job.
        f. Always use a cutting board.
        g. Always wear protective cutting gloves when using sharp knives.
        h. Remove lids completely when opening cans.
6. Use oven mitts or potholders to handle hot kettles, pots and pans.
7. Use covers on food choppers, food processors, blenders and grinders; turn off and unplug before stirring food in processors and blenders. Use appropriate "pushers" to push food into grinders.
8. Use safety guard on slicer blade; use safety handle to move meats through slicer.
9. Keep handles of pots and pans turned away from the edge of the stove.
10. When removing lids from pots and pans, raise the far edge of the cover to direct the steam away from you.
11. Discard chipped or cracked glass or chinaware.
12. Clear a space to put hot materials down before removing them from the range.
13. Use power equipment cautiously. Keep guards in place. Make sure that attachments are secure.
14. Maintenance of electrical equipment is particularly important to employees working in wet areas.

SAFETY AND ACCIDENT PREVENTION MANAGEMENT A-4

E. Electrical Equipment
 1. All electrical equipment should be equipped with three-prong power cords and plugs or a separate ground wire.
 2. Electrical power cords should be in good condition with no missing insulation or frayed wires.
 3. Doors in high traffic areas should be furnished with view windows.
 4. Keep to the right when wheeling food carts in corridors.
 5. Do not attempt to push or pull food carts with wheels that do not rotate easily. Have them serviced or repaired.
 6. Do not overload trays with liquid containers.
 7. Do not let food carts block corridors or doorways.

F. Fire Prevention
 1. Keep range hoods and other cooking equipment clean and free from accumulated grease. Clean vents in range hoods on a regular basis.
 2. Report any gas odor to the Dietary Manager (DM) or the Maintenance Supervisor.
 3. Maintain switches, cords or electrical outlets in good repair.
 4. Smoking is permitted only in designated areas. Dispose of smoking materials in receptacles provided in this same area, not in wastebaskets.
 5. Learn the location and use of fire extinguishers and the fire-reporting system in the facility.

CLEANING AND SANITATION PROCEDURES B

INTRODUCTION

The dining services department is part of the total resident care. The primary purpose of the department is to provide wholesome, safe, and appetizing food that meets the nutritional, psychosocial, and psychological needs of the resident according to the physician's diet order, as well as complying with local, state, and federal requirements and this facility' quality standards and service. To fulfil the department's purpose, a state of cleanliness must be maintained at all times.

If food-preparation areas are not cleaned frequently, there is a high risk of food contamination and spread of germs. If kitchen equipment, utensils, and dishware are not properly cleaned and sanitized, dangerous levels of bacteria could be spread throughout the facility, causing illness, infection, or even death.

Cleanliness in the dining services department is serious business, and it is the responsibility of every dining services department staff member to ensure that all aspects of the food-preparation area are kept clean and maintained to standards.

The cleaning procedures included in this chapter are simple and easy to follow. They have been developed and tested in long-term care facilities by this author and the staff. Besides being simply written and easy to understand, they are efficient, time and cost effective and safe when followed.

FOOD THERMOMETER CALIBRATION   B-1

1. Fill a large glass with crushed ice and clean tap water and stir.

2. Place the thermometer stem into the water submerging about half an inch above the groove without touching the glass bottom or sides.

3. Wait fifteen (15) seconds or until the indicator stops moving.

4. <u>Bi-Metallic Stemmed Thermometer</u>: With the stem in the ice water, hold the adjusting nut under the head of the thermometer and move the thermometer head so that the pointer reads 32 °F.

5. <u>Digital Thermometer</u>: With the stem in the ice water, push the reset button until the readout adjusts itself.

Boiling Water Method   **Cold Water Method**

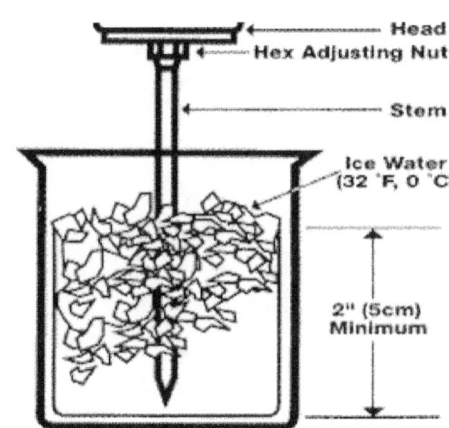

CLEANING OF DINING AREAS   B-2

All dining areas will be cleaned before meals are served and between seatings.

PROCEDURE

1. Tables will be bussed by the CNAs before escorting residents away from the tables and out of the dining room area.

2. Housekeeping will routinely clean the dining room once all residents leave.

3. If Dietary employees assist in the cleaning of the dining room, they must use housekeeping mops and supplies and ensure there is no cross-contamination brought into the kitchen.

4. Dietary cleaning equipment, such as: brooms, mops and cleaning cloths, will not be used in resident areas to avoid cross-contamination.

CLEANING OF CAN OPENER AND BASE B-3

Proper sanitation and maintenance of the can opener and base is important to sanitary food preparation. Metal shavings and shredding can result from a dull cutting blade or worn out cogwheel.

1. The can opener must be thoroughly cleaned after using.

2. Wash handle portion of the can opener in dish machine.

3. Wash the base with a brush and a detergent solution to keep seam area clean.

4. Unscrew base weekly to clean underneath

5. Make sure the shaft cavity is clean.

    a. Wash shaft daily and dry thoroughly before replacing.

    b. Apply food safe oil weekly to shaft cavity to keep from rusting.

    c. If shaft is rusty remove rust or replace shaft.

6. Return the clean opener to the base.

7. At least once every three (3) months the underside of the base should be cleaned, as well as the area on the table where the base rests.

8. Replace blade as needed. Dull blades may cause metal shards to drop inside the food when can is opened.

WALLS AND CEILINGS   B-4

1. Walls and ceilings must be free of chipped and/or peeling paint.

2. Walls and ceilings must be washed thoroughly at least twice each year. Heavily soiled surfaces must be cleaned more frequently and as required. It is important to repair peeling paint areas as soon as they appear.

3. The type of surface will determine the type of detergent and cleaning method.

4. Painted walls and ceilings should be washed with a mild detergent solution, rinsed using a clean cloth and dried to eliminate streaking.

5. Ceramic tile, stainless steel sections, and other surfaces must be cleaned according to product manufacturer's instructions.

SHELVES, COUNTERTOPS AND OTHER SURFACES   B-5

1. Wash surface with a warm detergent solution. Use a brush where necessary. To avoid scratching the surface, **do not** use metal scouring pads on stainless steel.

2. Rinse with clear water using a clean sponge or cloth.

3. Wipe dry with a dry cloth.

4. May use stainless steel polish to minimize finger marks and improve the appearance of stainless steel surfaces, such as refrigerator doors.

5. <u>Wooden Tables</u>

    a. Wash with warm detergent solution, using long even strokes.

    b. Rinse with clean water. Apply sanitizing solution with a clean sponge. Wipe off excess solution and allow to air dry.

6. <u>Cutting Boards</u>

    a. Cutting boards must be sanitized after each use, including after using for raw food and before using for cooked food. Wash with warm detergent solution. Rinse with clean water.

    b. Apply sanitizing solution with a clean sponge.

    c. Use separate cutting boards for raw and cooked foods to prevent cross-contamination with bacteria.

    <u>Note</u>: Wooden counters **are not** to be used for cutting. Seal unfinished wood counters sealed with Varathane. Do not cut directly on stainless steel counters as this dulls and chips knives.

SHELVES, COUNTERTOPS AND OTHER SURFACES   B-5

1. Wash surface with a warm detergent solution. Use a brush where necessary. To avoid scratching the surface, **do not** use metal scouring pads on stainless steel.

2. Rinse with clear water using a clean sponge or cloth.

3. Wipe dry with a dry cloth.

4. May use stainless steel polish to minimize finger marks and improve the appearance of stainless steel surfaces, such as refrigerator doors.

5. <u>Wooden Tables</u>

    a. Wash with warm detergent solution, using long even strokes.

    b. Rinse with clean water. Apply sanitizing solution with a clean sponge. Wipe off excess solution and allow to air dry.

6. <u>Cutting Boards</u>

    a. Cutting boards must be sanitized after each use, including after using for raw food and before using for cooked food. Wash with warm detergent solution. Rinse with clean water.

    b. Apply sanitizing solution with a clean sponge.

    c. Use separate cutting boards for raw and cooked foods to prevent cross-contamination with bacteria.

    <u>Note</u>: Wooden counters **are not** to be used for cutting. Seal unfinished wood counters sealed with Varathane. Do not cut directly on stainless steel counters as this dulls and chips knives.

CLEANING OF FLOORS   B-6

PROCEDURE

1. Floors should be mopped after each meal.

2. Sweep the floor, pushing all debris forward. Use a dust pan to remove debris as it accumulates.

3. Prepare detergent water (with germicidal cleaner recommended for the floor being cleaned) according to the manufacturer's instructions. Use a two-compartment mop bucket which has a mop press.

4. All mobile equipment should be removed from area being mopped.

5. Mop a small area at a time, begin at the rear of the room.

6. Change mop and water when either becomes gray.

7. Mop the floor in a figure eight movement. Use a scraper to remove stubborn stains.

8. Mop under and around equipment, along walls and in corners. Wipe all splash and soil marks from baseboards and walls.

9. Rinse the area with clean water.

10. Use **caution** signs on wet floors. The wet floor should not be walked on until it is thoroughly dry.

11. Wipe up all spills as they occur.

12. Clean as you go.

CLEANING OF COFFEE BREWING EQUIPMENT   B-7

Coffee urns and coffee service equipment must be free of stains and foreign film build-up.

Caution: Urn cleaners and other detergents must be used with caution. Follow product manufacturer's instructions.

PROCEDURE

- A. Coffee Urn
    1. Cleaning Procedure
        a. Remove the coffee basket as soon as the coffee is brewed and the basket has drained completely. Dispose of coffee grounds. Wash basket immediately.
        b. Empty the coffee urn after each meal.
        c. A potential health hazard exists if coffee is brewed in the urn before it is adequately rinsed out after being cleaned.
    2. Safety Procedure
        a. Hang warning sign on the urn (**Warning: DO NOT USE**).
        b. Empty urn.
        c. Rinse urn thoroughly with hot water.
        d. To remove discoloration, clean the urn with a mild detergent, baking soda or with an urn cleaner.
        e. Rinse urn thoroughly first with hot, then with cold water.
        f. Clean gauges each time the urn is cleaned.
        g. Pour one (1) gallon of fresh water into the urn after it is thoroughly rinsed. This will prevent the urn jacket from burning out. Adjust the thermostat to a position recommended by the manufacturer.
        h. Clean the exterior of the urn.
        i. Cean the urn cabinet stand, shelves and under the drain grating daily.
- B. Coffee Pot Destaining
    - a. Soak each coffee pot a minimum of twice each week, using an appropriate destaining solution.
    - b. Follow the detergent manufacturer's instructions for proper application of the cleaning product.

CLEANING OF COFFEE BREWING EQUIPMENT   B-7

- C. Automatic Drip Coffee Maker
  - a. <u>After each meal</u>:
    - i. Remove coffee grounds immediately after the water has dripped through. Rinse filters and bowls with clear, hot water.
    - ii. Wash serving decanters in dish machine.
    - iii. Wipe underside of spray head on coffee maker with a clean, damp sponge.
    - iv. Wash all metal surfaces with a sponge and detergent solution. Rinse and dry.
  - b. <u>Three times weekly</u>:
    Wash decanters, metal brewing cartridges in an urn cleaner solution. Do not use scouring abrasive powders on glass decanters as they will scratch the surface. Rinse thoroughly.

- D. Operate the machine using brewing cartridges and decanter at least one cycle without coffee to remove any trace of urn cleaner.

MONITORING DISHWASHING MACHINES   B-8

All dishwashing machines will be monitored on a routine basis for safe and acceptable temperatures and sanitizer concentration to ensure operation at established standards and to prevent contamination.

PROCEDURES

- A. Checking Wash Temperature
    1. Remove scrap tray.
    2. Insert holding thermometer in wash water for ten (10) seconds.
    3. <u>Conventional (hot water sanitizing) machines</u>: Preferred wash temperature is 160°F - 180°F depending on the manufacturer.
    4. <u>Low temperature (chemical sanitizing) machine</u>: Minimum acceptable wash temperature should conform to that indicated on the machine label, usually 120°F - 140°F.
    5. Record on Daily Temperature and Sanitizer Record.

- B. Checking Final Rinse Temperature (Conventional Machines)
    1. Run the machine empty at least one full wash/rinse cycle before checking temperature.
    2. Place holding thermometer in the center of an empty silverware tray, on a slant if possible. Anchor in place with a fork, secure in place with a rubber band attached to an inverted glass or cup. Run machine through another cycle.
    3. Holding thermometer should reach at least 170°F. Temperatures below 170°F are not acceptable. Current regulations and National Sanitation Foundation Standards for conventional machines require that water must reach the manifold of the final rinse section at 180°F. The water, however, passes through several inches of pipe, spray jets and air space between the manifold and the dishes, and is subject to some cooling. NSF standards and regulations are met when the holding temperature is at least 170°F, indication that the manifold temperature is at least 180°F.
    4. Record on Daily Temperature Record.

- C. Checking Concentration of Chemical Sanitizer (Low Temperature Machines)
    1. Run the dishmachine empty through the complete cycle.

MONITORING DISHWASHING MACHINES   B-8

       2.   Run the machine again, permitting the sanitizing rinse to start automatically. At the end of the cycle, test a sample of rinse water remaining in the tank with a test kit. Follow instructions given on the kit. Thio-sulfate titration is the preferred method of testing; starch-iodine papers are acceptable for a "quick test".

       3.   Record on Daily Temperature and Sanitizer Record for Dishmachines.

D.   Checking Final Rinse Pressure
1. Run machine.
2. Visually check the pressure gauge during the final rinse cycle, to be sure that the final rinse pressure is at least equal to that indicated on the NSF engraved plate attached to the front or side of the machine.
3. Record on Daily Temperature Record.

E.   If any of the aforementioned test results do not meet acceptable standards, dishwashing personnel will:
1. Check all dials and gauges to ascertain that they are set correctly. Check the quantity of chemical sanitizer in the container, if applicable.
2. Notify the Dietary Manager.
3. If the Dietary Manager is not available, notify the relief Supervisor or the Cook in charge, or the Maintenance Department.
4. If chemical/sanitation supplies are provided by a contract service company, follow designated procedures established with that company.

F.   The Dietary Manager is responsible for instructing all dishwashing employees in the importance of proper dishwashing machine temperatures, final rinse water pressure and, if a low temperature machine is in use, the proper concentration of chemical sanitizer.

Note: Before implementing and following these guidelines, check the manufacturer's recommendations and instructions from your dishmachine company.

(Insert the appropriate instructions for the brand of dishmachine and chemicals used in your facility in this section)

MONITORING DISHWASHING MACHINES   B-8

All dishwashing machines will be monitored on a routine basis for safe and acceptable temperatures and sanitizer concentration to ensure operation at established standards and to prevent contamination.

PROCEDURES

    A.   Checking Wash Temperature
          1.   Remove scrap tray.
          2.   Insert holding thermometer in wash water for ten (10) seconds.
          3.   <u>Conventional (hot water sanitizing) machines</u>: Preferred wash temperature is 160°F - 180°F depending on the manufacturer.
          4.   <u>Low temperature (chemical sanitizing) machine</u>: Minimum acceptable wash temperature should conform to that indicated on the machine label, usually 120°F - 140°F.
          5.   Record on Daily Temperature and Sanitizer Record.

    B.   Checking Final Rinse Temperature (Conventional Machines)
          1.   Run the machine empty at least one full wash/rinse cycle before checking temperature.
          2.   Place holding thermometer in the center of an empty silverware tray, on a slant if possible. Anchor in place with a fork, secure in place with a rubber band attached to an inverted glass or cup. Run machine through another cycle.
          3.   Holding thermometer should reach at least 170°F. Temperatures below 170°F are not acceptable. Current regulations and National Sanitation Foundation Standards for conventional machines require that water must reach the manifold of the final rinse section at 180°F. The water, however, passes through several inches of pipe, spray jets and air space between the manifold and the dishes, and is subject to some cooling. NSF standards and regulations are met when the holding temperature is at least 170°F, indication that the manifold temperature is at least 180°F.
          4.   Record on Daily Temperature Record.

    C.   Checking Concentration of Chemical Sanitizer (Low Temperature Machines)
          1.   Run the dishmachine empty through the complete cycle.

MONITORING DISHWASHING MACHINES   B-8

    2.   Run the machine again, permitting the sanitizing rinse to start automatically. At the end of the cycle, test a sample of rinse water remaining in the tank with a test kit. Follow instructions given on the kit. Thio-sulfate titration is the preferred method of testing; starch-iodine papers are acceptable for a "quick test".
    3.   Record on Daily Temperature and Sanitizer Record for Dishmachines.

D.   Checking Final Rinse Pressure
    1.   Run machine.
    2.   Visually check the pressure gauge during the final rinse cycle, to be sure that the final rinse pressure is at least equal to that indicated on the NSF engraved plate attached to the front or side of the machine.
    3.   Record on Daily Temperature Record.

E.   If any of the aforementioned test results do not meet acceptable standards, dishwashing personnel will:
    1.   Check all dials and gauges to ascertain that they are set correctly. Check the quantity of chemical sanitizer in the container, if applicable.
    2.   Notify the Dietary Manager.
    3.   If the Dietary Manager is not available, notify the relief Supervisor or the Cook in charge, or the Maintenance Department.
    4.   If chemical/sanitation supplies are provided by a contract service company, follow designated procedures established with that company.

F.   The Dietary Manager is responsible for instructing all dishwashing employees in the importance of proper dishwashing machine temperatures, final rinse water pressure and, if a low temperature machine is in use, the proper concentration of chemical sanitizer.

Note: Before implementing and following these guidelines, check the manufacturer's recommendations and instructions from your dishmachine company.

(Insert the appropriate instructions for the brand of dishmachine and chemicals used in your facility in this section)

GENERAL DISHROOM SANITATION B-9

Food waste material, heat and moisture are the primary contributors to unsanitary conditions in the Dietary Services Department and all are present in the dishroom.

- A. <u>Dish Racks</u> - Dish racks must be handled and stored off the floor. Both full and empty dish racks are to be stored on a dish rack dolly cart or an undershelf in the dishroom at all times. Generally, the floor has a high bacterial contamination and is not considered to be a clean area.

- B. <u>Work Surfaces</u> - Dishroom work surfaces must be maintained in a clean and sanitary condition.
    1. Wash the soiled dish table, rinse and dry.
    2. Wipe down the exterior of the dish machine; give particular attention to the top of the machine.
    3. Wipe down all other work surfaces in the dishroom.

- C. <u>Dishware</u> - Chips and cracks in dishware provide a home for bacteria and a potential contamination source. It can also be a safety hazard to residents and employees.
    1. The dish machine operator should sort out chipped and/or cracked dishware, including trays and plate covers.
    2. The Dietary Service Supervisor examines the sorted items to determine whether or not they meet acceptable standards. If not, damaged ware shall be discarded and replaced.

- D. <u>Plastic ware</u> – Plastic utensils are considered to be inferior if not stain free and immaculately clean.
    1. Consult your dish machine detergent supplier for their recommendations on a plastic destainer.
    2. Establish routine schedules for destaining plastic. Be sure to define how, by whom and when the procedure will be carried out.
    3. Daily examination of plastic ware (by random sample), will ensure acceptability.
    4. Do not use metal sponges or green scrubbies on plastic ware.

MACHINE DISHWASHING, DRYING AND STORAGE   B-10

All service ware will be washed, sanitized, air-dried and stored after each use utilizing established standards of sanitation.

PROCEDURES

A. Dishwashing Machine
1. At least two (2) employees should operate the dish machine to prevent cross-contamination; one to handle soiled dishes, and one to handle clean dishes.
2. When there is only one (1) employee, a strict handwashing routine shall be followed each time the employee moves from the soiled to the clean dish area.
3. Scraping and Pre-Rinse
    a. Sort and separate flatware, glasses and dishes.
    b. Flatware should be pre-soaked in a deep pan of water with detergent.
    c. Pre-soak dishes if necessary.
    d. Stack trays.
4. Racking
    a. Rack without overlapping in appropriate rack. Do not overload.
    b. Rack cups, bowls, and glasses upside down.
    c. Flatware should be spread in a thin layer in a rack, or can be sorted and placed loosely in cylinders with handles down. One empty cylinder should be washed with each batch of flatware. This permits inverting the clean flatware into clean cylinders so that handles   point up and mouth-pieces are not handled.

5. Washing and Sanitizing
    a. Conventional (hot water sanitizing) Machines
        - Add detergent according to instructions.
        - If there is no automatic dispenser, at least one (1) tablespoon of detergent must be added with every other rack.

MACHINE DISHWASHING, DRYING AND STORAGE   B-10

- Check water temperature. The preferred wash temperature: 160°F -165°F; minimum acceptable: 145°F. Sanitizer rinse temperature rinse cycle: 180°F.

   b. Low Temperature (chemical sanitizing) Machines
   - Check the automatic detergent and rinsing agent dispensers. Both should be operable during the wash/rinse cycle.
   - Check water temperature. Minimum acceptable temperature should conform to that indicated on the machine label, usually 140°F.

   6. All Machines
      a. Do not pull racks through the automatic machines.
      b. Water pressure and volume must be sufficient to wash all parts of the dishes. The wash arm openings and rinse spray nozzles must be kept clean.
      c. Clean after each meal service.

B. Drying
   1. All items will be air dried before stacking and storing.
   2. Do not use dishtowels to dry.

D. Storage
   1. Clean, dry dishes should be stored above the floor in a clean, dry place, protected from contamination.
   2. Cups and glasses should be stored upside down.
   3. Avoid handling surfaces which will come in contact with food or mouth.
   4. Discard cracked or chipped dishes.

D. Disposables
   1. Disposable single service items must be discarded after each use, and are not to be returned to the Dietary Department for sanitation.

MANUAL DISHWASHING   B-11

POLICY

Utensils that must be cleaned manually will be washed, rinsed, sanitized and dried using established sanitation criteria.

PROCEDURES

    A.   <u>Three-Compartment Method</u>

        1.   Wash in hot water (110°F-120°F) with an effective detergent in proper concentration. Water should be changed frequently.

        2.   Rinse in clean, clear, hot water. Change water frequently.

        3.   Sanitize by submerging in hot water (180°F) for thirty (30) seconds or use a chemical as directed and approved by the State Department of Public Health. Wire baskets are essential for immersing dishes in 180°F water. The water must be changed when cloudy.

        4.   Air dry on a drain board. Dishtowels should not be used.

        5.   Inspect and store on clean, dry, protected shelves.

THREE-COMPARTMENT METHOD

Drain board	Compartment		
	1	2	3
Stacked Pre-rinsed	Wash	Rinse	Sanitize

MANUAL DISHWASHING   B-11

B. <u>Two-Compartment Method</u>

1. Scrape and pre-rinse soiled utensils.

2. Wash in hot water (110°F-120°F) with an effective detergent in the proper concentration. Water should be changed frequently.

3. Rinse by submerging the utensils in clean water (180°F) for at least thirty (30) seconds, or use a chemical as directed and approved by the State Department of Health.

4. Air-dry on a drain board. Dishtowels should not be used.

5. Inspect and store on clean, dry, protected shelves.

TWO-COMPARTMENT METHOD

Drain board	Compartment		
	1	2	2
Stacked Pre-rinsed	**Wash**	**Rinse**	**Refill with clean water & sanitizer Sanitize**

DISPENSING EQUIPMENT

B-12

JUICE DISPENSER

1. Remove nozzles and diffusers and soak them in warm soapy water daily.

2. Wipe exterior surfaces with soap and water after each meal.

    - Do not use caustic cleaners or chlorine as they may cause stains, discoloration or rust.

3. Clean and flush water lines at least weekly.

4. Remove any trays or bins and wash weekly.

5. If there is an ice bin, empty and wash monthly.

6. Follow manufacturer's recommendations.

MILK DISPENSER

Milk provides an excellent medium for the growth of micro-organisms and it must be refrigerated (36°F-40°F) to control bacterial growth. The dispenser tubing must be no longer than one (1) inch in length, and cut at a forty-five degree (45°) angle in order to prevent milk from remaining in the tube and reaching room temperature.

   A. Milk dispensers are cleaned daily after each use and washed at least weekly.

    1. Remove milk containers from the dispenser to prepare for cleaning at least once a week. Place the containers in the refrigerator if they have any milk in them.

    2. Disconnect the electrical supply.

    3. Use a sponge to wash the interior of the dispenser with a detergent solution.

    4. Remove and dismantle the dispenser head. Wash it in a detergent solution, rinse and let air dry.

DISPENSING EQUIPMENT B-12

MILK DISPENSER (cont)

5. Special attention must be given to washing, rinsing, and air drying of the rubber seal on the door, the edge of door, the thermometer, and the corners and hinges.

6. Wash and rinse the exterior of the dispenser.

7. Polish the exterior of the dispenser with the polish recommended by the manufacturer.

8. Reconnect the electrical supply. **Do not return the milk containers to the dispenser until the temperature of the dispenser reaches 40°F.**

9. To catch overflow and leakage, place a tray under the faucets.

10. Follow manufacturer's recommendations.

DRY STORAGE AREAS   B-13

A. General cleanliness and care of the storeroom and supplies are important to ensure good, wholesome food.

B. The floor, walls, ceiling, lights, shelves and equipment in the storeroom will be kept clean by setting up, maintaining, and monitoring a regular cleaning schedule.

C. Conduct routine inspections of the storeroom to ensure cleanliness and high standards of sanitation.

D. Leaking or severely dented cans and spoiled foods should be disposed of promptly to prevent contamination of other foods. If damaged when delivered, return them to the purveyor for credit.

E. Transfer bulk staple items into metal or plastic containers with tight fitting covers to prevent insect or rodent infestation.

F. When products are removed from the original packaging it is important to label and date the container with the name of product, delivery and use by dates.

G. Food and supplies are stored 18" from ceiling and 6" from the floor.

H. If shelving is made of wood it must be sealed with a high gloss washable finish.

I. The recommended dry storage temperature is between 65°F and 75°F. However, the temperature inside the store room should not exceed 85°F to prevent deterioration and spoilage.

J. In areas of extreme heat, arrangements to cool down the dry storage areas is essential to maintain food safety.

K. Storage room should have sufficient lights and ventilation to prevent food deterioration and to ensure safe working conditions.

L. It is advisable to check local, state and federal guidelines and state and federal food codes.

M. Genearal guidelines for cleaning the dry storage areas:

DRY STORAGE AREAS   B-13

1. Clean floors daily at the end of each day by seeping and mopping floor.

2. Pick up dropped items clean up all spilled food on floors and shelves right away.

3. Weekly the day before groceries delivery, wipe all shelves, clean all dust from surfaces, inspect and reseal packages and storage bins, check expiration dates and remove expired foods.

4. Keep store room doors and windows shut to prevent vermin infestation.

ELECTRICAL FOOD MACHINES   B-14

Keep and maintain all food machines, including: mixers, grinders, slicers, and toasters in good operating and sanitary condition.

    A.   Mixing Machines
        1.   Wash bowl and beater after each use **(Caution: always unplug before cleaning.)**
        2.   If the food in the bowl is an egg or flour mixture, soak bowl in cold water before washing.
        3.   Clean the beater shaft and body of the machine with warm water and mild soap. Hard scrubbing and harsh soaps might remove the paint.
        4.   After washing and rinsing, allow beater to air dry, then store in the proper place.
        5.   Oil the motor and fill the grease cups as directed by the manufacturer.

    B.   Food Grinders
        1.   Wash after each use **(Caution: always unplug before cleaning.)**
        2.   Remove adjustment ring, knife and plate; wash in hot, soapy water; rinse and dry thoroughly.
        3.   Wash, rinse and dry other parts of the grinder.

    C.   Food Slicer
        1.   Clean the slicer after each use **(Caution: always unplug before cleaning.)**
        2.   Clean the knife blade carefully, wiping away from the cutting edge of the knife and guarding it from contact with other metal surfaces which could dull or nick the blade.
        3.   Use hot water, mild soap and a clean cloth to thoroughly wash the parts that come in contact with food. Wash or wipe other parts of the machine with a damp cloth; dry thoroughly. Avoid excessively hot water or steam (Too much heat can burn up the lubricants on the friction points).
        4.   Apply special food machine oil.

ELECTRICAL FOOD MACHINES   B-14

D. Automatic Toaster
1. Clean toaster after each use **(Caution: always unplug before cleaning.)**
2. Brush the crumbs from the interior, exercising care to avoid damage to the interior heating elements.
3. Remove the crumb tray. Wash, rinse and air dry.
4. Wash the exterior of the toaster with a sponge and detergent solution. Rinse with clear water. Do not allow water to penetrate the interior of the toaster. Wipe dry.
5. Return the crumb tray. Reconnect the plug. Clean all of surrounding area.

E. Rotary Toaster
1. Clean toaster after each use **(Caution: always unplug before cleaning.)**
2. Brush crumbs from the front of the surface of the toaster, and behind the bread racks.
3. Remove and wash the toast guide and crumb tray. Rinse and air dry. Exercise special care to avoid damaging the wires of the toast guide.
4. Wash the toaster frames, being careful not to allow water to penetrate the interior of the toaster. Rinse and wipe dry.
5. Clean the area underneath and surrounding the toaster.
6. Replace toast guide and tray. Reconnect the plug.

F. Ice Machine
1. Disconnect unit from electrical supply.
2. Drain ice from bin.
3. Wash interior with detergent solution. Absorb excess moisture with a sponge. Rinse with clean water and a separate sponge.
4. Apply sanitizing solution with a spray bottle. Allow to air dry.
5. Reconnect and start the unit.

Note: Please refer to the manufacturer's instructions for all equipment cleaning and repair.

PREVENTION OF RODENT INFESTATION   B-15

INSPECT THE AREA FOR THE FOLLOWING
- Droppings: Trails of roddent droppings along walls, on beams, wide ledges, top of wall studs & beams, window sills, , inside and around boxes and bags, under and around racks, wedged in the corners
- Gnaw marks: Usually in the corners of cardboard and light plastic boxes, any part of a paper or plastic sack, plastic wrap covering baked goods in store room or walk-in refrigerator
- Dark places such as insulation where they burrow, grain sacks, flour, sugar
- Boxes: potatoes, bananas, apples
- Damaged food packages regardless of the type of food

TO PROTECT AND PREVENT RODENT INFESTATION
1. Contact professional exterminator service immediately
2. Thoroughly inspect all areas inside and outside of each building inspecting for holes in the walls, roof and celiling, open exhaust pipes on roof, holes leading to water pipes such as under sinks and fawcetts.
3. Crevices underneath all doors especially those leading to outside and from facility into kichen
4. Focus on food deliver and storage areas, refuse disposal areas, laundry rooms and equipment rooms. Any dark enclosed areas
5. Examine all screens for even the smallest holes or openings
6. Roof and vents
7. Keep all exterior refuse containers covered and area around them clean.

HOODS, VENTS AND FILTERS   B-16

A. Hoods
 1. Clean every two (2) weeks to keep free of dust and grease.
 2. Wash hood with detergent solution using a brush, sponge or cloth.
 3. Remove the filters and wash the retainer brackets. Wash the hood grease trench with a detergent solution, using a brush, sponge or cloth.
 4. Rinse the hood with hot water. Absorb excess water with sponge or cloth.
 5. Polish hood with stainless steel polish using a paper towel or cloth.

B. Filters
 1. Hood filters will be washed weekly to decrease fire hazard.
 2. Remove filters from hood.
 3. Soak filters in a solution of ½ cup of Tri-Sodium Phosphate to fifteen (15) gallons of water.
 4. Wash by passing each filter through the dish machine. Lay one filter flat on the dish rack. Do not stack filters.
 5. Allow filters to air dry before returning to hood.
 6. Hood light fixtures must be cleaned every two (2) weeks. Hood lights must have protective guards over them and be in good operating condition.

C. Hood Shafts
 1. Hood exhaust shafts will be cleaned by a contract maintenance service company to maintain safety and meet local fire code requirements.
 2. Service records will be kept for one (1) year.

HOT FOOD TABLES, TRAY CARTS AND SHELVES   B-17

A. <u>Hot Food Table</u>

The hot food table is also called a steamtable. The hot food table determines the final quality and temperature of hot foods served. The cleanliness and proper function of the hot food table are vital to maintaining appropriate temperatures of hot food wells.

1. Hot food table wells must be kept clean and free of scale in order to ensure proper food temperatures and food wholesomeness.
2. Hot food wells should be cleaned after each meal.
3. Food spillage must be removed immediately to avoid carbonized areas on the hot table.
4. The water must be changed daily in wet hot table wells.
5. The addition of 1/8 cup (one ounce) of lime and scale remover per gallon of clean water in each well will help prevent scaling. **A stronger solution is not recommended.** Lime and scale remover is available from your dish machine detergent supplier.

<u>Wet-Type Tables</u>
1. Remove the food pans from the table.
2. Turn off heat; allow the table to cool.
3. Drain the wells, if equipped with a drain. If not, sponge out, rinse and dry the wells.
4. Wash the exterior of the table with a detergent solution, rinse and dry.
5. Polish the stainless surfaces of the table.
6. Add 1/8 cup (one ounce) of descaling solution per gallon of water when refilling the wells.

<u>Dry Tables</u>
1. Remove the food pans from the table.
2. Turn off heat, allow the table to cool.
3. Scrape food spillage from inside of well. If spillage has carbonized, use a damp metal sponge to remove it. Spray with carbon remover if necessary before using sponge. Wipe clean with a clean cloth or sponge.
4. Polish the stainless steel surfaces of the table.

<u>Caution</u>: Do not allow water to come in contact with the heating elements.

<u>Thermostats</u>
1. The thermostat on the hot table must operate properly at all times. Report all defective controls and equipment to the Dietary Manager.

HOT FOOD TABLES, TRAY CARTS AND SHELVES B-17

B. Meal and Tray Delivery Carts
1. Keep all food carts thoroughly clean at all times. Establish a routine cleaning schedule based on the following standards:
2. Carts must be wiped clean after each meal. Using mild germicidal solution (1 ounce bleach to 1 gallon water) and a sponge, wipe the inside and outside of each cart, rinse and allow to air dry.
3. Carts must be washed completely each week and as often as soiled.
   - Take the cart to the cart-wash area.
   - Using a mild detergent solution and brush, scrub the cart inside and outside.
   - Scrub the wheels.
   - Rinse well and allow to dry.
   - Use appropriate cleaners or polish on exterior walls to preserve the finish.
4. Oil casters periodically to ensure smooth operation.

C. Shelves and Surfaces
   <u>Surfaces</u>
   1. All surfaces must be thoroughly cleaned at least once daily.
   2. Stainless steel polish should be applied as directed.
   <u>Shelves</u>
   1. The under shelves of the tray assembly area must be kept clean and free of litter. A routine schedule should be posted designating the frequency of cleaning and by whom.
   2. Remove all items from the under shelves.
   4. If the shelves are removable, take them to the pot and pan wash area, wash them in detergent water, rinse and air dry.
   5. Clean the under shelf area with a mild detergent solution, rinse and dry.
   6. Return the shelves to their proper position.
   7. Return the stored items to the shelves, arranging them neatly.

CLEANING OF ICE MACHINES B-18

Follow manufacturer's instructions and recommended cleaning procedures for all ice machines.

- A. Outside of ice machine is cleaned daily with warm soapy water, then rinsed and allowed to air dry.

- B. Inside bin of ice machine is cleaned weekly per manufacturer's recommendations.

- C. If there are no recommendations available, the following is recommended:

    1. Empty ice bin completely and discard ice.

    2. Clean inside of bin with warm soapy water or other food safe cleaner recommended for interior of ice machine bin.

    3. Rinse thoroughly until no residue remains.

    4. Wipe bin with a mild bleach solution of ¾ cup chlorine bleach to one (1) gallon of warm water.

    5. Air dry, then close to restart ice making process.

- D. Check ice machines daily to ensure ice is not melting, that enough ice is produced and other signs of malfunction.

CLEANING OF ICE MACHINES   B-18

ICE MAKER MANUFACTURER INSTRUCTIONS

Include a copy of the ice maker manufacturer's instructions manual in this section.

- Ice maker manufacturer _____
- Model name _____
- Model number_____
- Serial number _____
- Date purchased (if available) _____
- Repair service number _____

CLEANING AND STORAGE OF ICE SCOOP

1. Store ice scoop outside of the ice or ice machine in an appropriate covered container.

2. Wash scoop daily.

3. Label the ice container with the date scoop is returned to container.

4. When ice is needed from the machine, only the ice scoop will be used for dispensing. The ice scoop will then be immediately replaced in its covered storage place.

5. Do not hold containers being filled inside the ice machine. Use separate cart or tray outside of the ice machine to prevent ice from contamination.

INGREDIENT BINS   B-19

1. Keep ingredient bins clean, labeled and covered to prevent food contamination.

2. Scrub the interior and exterior of empty bins with detergent solution. Pay special attention to the corners, lids and casters.

3. Rinse bins with clean water.

4. Invert bins upside-down off the floor and allow to air dry.

5. Restock bins after completely air dried.

6. Scoops used in bins must **not** be left in the bins. Scoops are washed daily.

7. Never refill bins without removing older products and cleaning thoroughly.

STORAGE OF CLEANING SUPPLIES AND JANITOR'S CLOSET   B-20

JANITORIAL CLOSETS & ROOMS AND CLEANING SUPPLIES STORAGE & HANDLING

1. The janitor's closet must be kept clean and orderly.
2. After each use, all equipment must be cleaned and rinsed before storage.
3. Mops must be washed, rinsed, wrung out and allowed to air dry before returning to the janitor's closet.
    a. Storage outside of the kitchen is acceptable, but caution is required to prevent cross-contamination by vermin.
        i. Watch for flies resting on mops, larvae breeding on stagnant or held water.
        ii. Use hooks to hang mops and brooms, do not rest them on the floor or ground.
    b. Mops used in the Dietary Services Department are for the exclusive use inside the Department and never used in the resident areas, including the Dining Rooms.
    c. Mop heads should be washed separately from any other mops used in the common areas of the facility.
4. The mop bucket must be thoroughly scrubbed inside and out with detergent solution, rinsed, inverted and air dried before being returned to the janitor's closet.
5. Cleaning of the janitor's closet must be on a scheduled routine.
    a. <u>Weekly</u>
        i. Shelves, hooks and brush racks.
        ii. Walls and baseboards.
    b. <u>Daily</u>
        i. Janitor's sink cleaned.
        ii. Floor swept and mopped.
6. Detergents and cleaning agents must be stored at least five (5) inches of the floor. This prevents the products from becoming damp and hardened when detergents are stored in containers that are subject to moisture absorption.
    a. Detergents and cleaning agents must never be stored in the food store room or left in the kitchen when not in use.

MOPS AND MOP BUCKETS B-21

HANDLING AND STORAGE OF MOPS AND BUCKETS

1. Mops must be washed, rinsed, sanitized, wrung out and allowed to air dry. Do not store wet mops in the janitor's closet. It is recommended to keep three (3) clean mops on hand at all times.

2. Mop buckets and press must be emptied, scrubbed inside and out with a detergent solution, rinsed and allowed to air dry daily after last use.

3. Store the floor care equipment in its designated place.

4. Mops and buckets used in Dietary are dedicated exclusively to the Department and not used in any other part of the facility.

5. Mop heads used in Dietary must be washed separately from other mop heads used in the facility.

PEST CONTROL AND MONITORING B-22

1. All doors and windows must be properly screened.

2. In high fly areas, fly fans and other controls should be used.

3. Food must be properly covered and stored.

4. Do not use sprays and insecticides in food preparation areas. These must be applied by a licensed professional service.

5. If fly swatters are allowed in your state and county to kill stray insects entering the kitchen area unexpectedly such as during food deliveries, they will need to be sanitized after each use in a desginated area and stored in the janitor's closet.

6. The Dietary Services Department must be kept free of soil and clutter.

7. Arrangements should be made by the facility for a pest control firm to provide routine service.

CLEANING OF RANGES AND OVENS B-23

A. Ranges
1. Open top gas range and grill. When top grids are completely cool, remove them from the range and soak them in a solution of water and grease solvent. Remove encrusted material with a blunt scraper.
2. Boil grates and burners in salt/soda or other grease solvent/water solution. Clean clogged burner posts with a stiff wire brush.
3. Back splash apron and other large surfaces should be washed with a hot detergent solution to remove grease, rinse and dry with a clean cloth.
4. Range drip pans must be emptied and washed on a routinely scheduled basis after each use.
5. Grills must be cleaned after each use. Allow sufficient time for grills to cool before cleaning. Do not use caustic or acid solutions on grills as their use will eventually cause sticking and rusting.
    a. Use a blunt scraper, then wipe clean.
    b. Periodically use a grill or pumice stone with cooking oil and scrub until grill is clean. Wipe grill with a clean cloth.
    c. Always empty and wash the grease catch pan after each use.

B. Ovens and Broilers
1. Allow sufficient time for ovens to cool before cleaning.
2. Quarterly, racks and shelves should be removed and cleaned in a warm detergent solution.
3. Use a blunt scraper or wire brush to remove encrusted material from oven surface.
4. When a commercial oven cleaner is used, allow for ample ventilation and follow label directions.
5. Clean the exterior of the oven/broiler according to manufacturer's instructions.

CLEANING OF REFRIGERATORS AND FREEZERS – DIETARY

B-24

1. Clean refrigerators regularly according to the posted cleaning schedule.

2. Wash shelves and walls with warm water and a detergent. Scour with a stiff brush if necessary. Rinse with a weak solution of baking soda and water to eliminate any smells. Dry thoroughly.

3. Clean gaskets and inspect for mold and tears. Dry after cleaning. Report any tears or cracks to the Dietary Manager.

4. Mop floors in walk-in refrigeration equipment daily.

5. At least quarterly the drain pipes must be removed and flushed with hot water and soda.

6. Mop walk-in freezer with an approved freezer compound.

7. Store food off the floor on rolling dollies or raised shelves. Upside down milk crates are not allowed.

8. Store bulky items on the bottom shelves.

9. Keep freezer elements frost build-up. To obtain maximum results, the elements should be checked daily and defrosted as necessary.

10. Check thermometers routinely. Every refrigerator and freezer must have a thermometer and temperature logs maintained.

11. Monitor and record refrigerator and freezer temperatures. Report high or low temperatures as soon as noted.

CLEANING OF REFRIGERATORS AND FREEZERS – DIETARY

B-24

1. Clean refrigerators regularly according to the posted cleaning schedule.

2. Wash shelves and walls with warm water and a detergent. Scour with a stiff brush if necessary. Rinse with a weak solution of baking soda and water to eliminate any smells. Dry thoroughly.

3. Clean gaskets and inspect for mold and tears. Dry after cleaning. Report any tears or cracks to the Dietary Manager.

4. Mop floors in walk-in refrigeration equipment daily.

5. At least quarterly the drain pipes must be removed and flushed with hot water and soda.

6. Mop walk-in freezer with an approved freezer compound.

7. Store food off the floor on rolling dollies or raised shelves. Upside down milk crates are not allowed.

8. Store bulky items on the bottom shelves.

9. Keep freezer elements frost build-up. To obtain maximum results, the elements should be checked daily and defrosted as necessary.

10. Check thermometers routinely. Every refrigerator and freezer must have a thermometer and temperature logs maintained.

11. Monitor and record refrigerator and freezer temperatures. Report high or low temperatures as soon as noted.

CLEANING OF REFRIGERATORS - RESIDENT ROOMS B-25

Refrigerators refrigerators in residents' rooms are monitored routinely to comply with food safety and sanitation.

PROCEDURE

1. Personal refrigerators are listed in the resident inventory.

2. The Housekeeping Department keeps a current list of rooms with residents' refrigerators.

3. Each refrigerator will have an inside thermometer and temperature is monitored and logged daily. The refrigerator temperature is maintained at or below 41°F. Any temperatures not in range will be immediately reported to the Maintenance Supervisor and family or responsible party for repairs. If the temperature is not maintained at 41°F or below, the resident and family are informed that food will be discarded.

4. The Dietary Manager inservices the Housekeeping staff and family members regarding food safety, the correct use of thermometer, correct refrigerator temperature guidelines and seven (7) day food discard safety rule.

5. All food in the refrigerator is labeled with the common name, delivery and open date. Once opened, food is discarded by day seven (7) or by the manufacturer's guideline. At the family or resident's option, this can be done by facility staff or removed by family.

6. Housekeeping cleans and sanitizes the refrigerators at least once a month or as required.

7. Housekeeping Supervisor will conduct at least monthly quality assurance audit of refrigerators to monitor adherence to procedure. Results will be reported in the Quality Assurance Committee.

   a. DM will conduct spot-checks during routine rounds and validate results.

SANITIZING CLOTHS IN RED SANITIZING BUCKETS   B-26

Prepare sanitizing buckets before starting food preparation. Use sanitizing solution to hold cleaning cloths in food preparation areas between use to prevent bacterial growth. Sanitizing solution is not used for cleaning food contact surfaces.

RED BUCKETS

How to prepare and use sanitizing (red) bucket:

1. Fill a one (1) gallon sanitizing bucket half-full with lukewarm water of at least 95°F.

2. Add one (1) ounce of quaternary ammonia solution (one [1] capful). Stir solution and mix. For quaternary ammonia in pre-measured dispensers add the indicated number of "pumps" into bucket directly from the dispenser.

3. Use sanitizing solution test strips to test PPM in prepared bucket for a goal of 200 PPM. If test strip has incorrect reading, discard water and prepare again correctly, then test PPM again. **To test sanitizing solution** remove small amount in a clean cup (disposable cups work well), and allow to cool to room temperature. Dip test strip and read. Hot water alters the strip sensitivity and the reading is inaccurate.

4. Place clean damp wiping cloth in the prepared sanitizer bucket. Store cloth in bucket at all times when not using. Do not store wet cloth on counters.

Note: Terrycloth towels neutralize Quat sanitizer and are too thick. If using terrycloth towels, limit the number to two (2) per bucket and test PPM every hour.

5. Store prepared sanitizing bucket in area away from food production and storage, equipment, and six (6) inches above floor (i.e. on shelf below counter).

6. To clean and sanitize food preparation areas and equipment: wring cloth, rinse with warm running water, use food safe cleaner/sanitizer, or warm soapy water to wipe down food contact and equipment surfaces.

SANITIZING CLOTHS IN RED SANITIZING BUCKETS   B-26

7. Rinse out dirty cloth under running water in sink after wiping down surfaces. Do not put cloth back in the sanitizing solution until it is rinsed and water squeezed out. Return cloth back to sanitizing bucket. **Do not** store cloth on counters.

8. Change sanitizing solution in bucket after four (4) hours, or when cloudy.

9. At the end of shift, empty sanitizer solution from bucket into designated drain and soiled cloths are discarded in the designated container.

10. Wash and sanitize red buckets; store dry, unused sanitizing buckets in appropriate designated area.

GREEN BUCKETS

Green buckets are used to mix fresh warm cleaning/sanitizing solutions. This water is changed after each use. Green buckets are washed, sanitized and allowed to dry. Cloths are not held in the wash water.

CLEANING OF STEAMERS AND STEAM KETTLES   B-27

STEAMERS AND STEAM KETTLES

1. Steam cooking equipment can be maintained effectively by careful planning, training and supervision. Equipment will be scheduled for regular cleaning to prevent accumulation of dirt and spilled food. The equipment will be kept in good repair, and will have regular routine water treatment.
2. Information about the operation, cleaning and care of steamers and steam kettles can be obtained from the manufacturer or from the local distributor.
3. <u>Kettles</u>
   a. Kettles should be washed immediately after each use. If not possible and food particles harden, fill the kettles with tap water and allow to soak until the food particles have softened.
   b. Wash following normal procedures.
   c. Wash both the interior and exterior with hot water and detergent.
   d. Scour when necessary.
   e. Rinse with clear, clean water and dry the exterior of the unit with a clean cloth.
4. <u>Steam Compartment Cookers</u>
   a. It is important that the manufacturer's instructions be followed on internal cleaning.
   b. Do not allow accumulation of food particles or hard water scale to collect inside the compartment.
   c. Dry water pan and interior. Flush and drain lines. Remove shelves and clean pan slides.
   d. Remove door gaskets and clean weekly.
   e. Remove filter (on top of unit) weekly. Soak in soapy water and rinse with clear water.

(Follow manufacturers' recommendations. If instructions are available, place a copy in your instructions manual or include with this book)

CLEANING OF REFRIGERATORS AND FREEZERS - NURSING UNITS AND PANTRIES   B-28

PATIENT REFRIGERATORS OUTSIDE OF THE KITCHEN

1. Assign department(s) and staff responsible for cleaning and maintaining the Nursing Units and pantry refrigerators clean and orderly.

2. Clean refrigerators regularly according to the posted cleaning schedule.

3. Wash shelves and walls with warm water and a detergent. Scour with a stiff brush if necessary. Rinse with a weak solution of baking soda and water to eliminate any smells. Dry thoroughly.

4. Clean gaskets and inspect for mold and tears. Dry after cleaning. Report any tears or cracks to the Maintenance Supervisor.

5. If kept in a separate room or pantry ensure that floors are clean and only patient food is kept in them. No medications, no staff food

6. Keep freezer elements frost build-up.

7. Check thermometers routinely. Every refrigerator and freezer must have a thermometer and the temperature logged daily.

8. Report high or low temperatures as soon as noted.

9. The Dietary Manager and Nursing Supervisor inspect the refrigerators and freezers for cleanliness and compliance weekly.

FORMS RECORDS AND LOGS   C

Forms are a convenient and efficient record keeping method. There are a variety of forms available in the next section to use as reference for the purpose of:

- Evaluating and quantifying systems efficacy
- Monitoring staff performance and completion of tasks
- Monitoring and quantifying compliance.

Forms are also available for download at http://www.flavorfulfortifiedfood.com

LIST OF FORMS, RECORDS & LOGS IN THIS SECTION

- Sanitation Review with Comments
- Cooling Log
- Cleaning Schedule – Schedules & Tasks
- Temperature Records – Cooking
- Temperatire Records – Deliveries
- Temperature Records – Freezers
- Temperature Records - Refrigerators
- Temperature Records – Cooking & Cooling
- Dishmachine Temperature & PPM log
- Temperature Records – Thermometer Calibration
- Refrigerator & Freezer Storage Temperatures
- Cleaning Schedule Assigments & Procedures
- Pre Meal Checklist
- Kitchen Cleaning Daily Assignments
- Kitchen Cleaning Weekly January to June Assignments
- Kitchen Cleaning Weekly Assignments July to December Assignments
- Kitchen Cleaning Monthly Assignments
- Production Schedules & Standards
- Hazard Analysis Table – Process
- Hazard Analysis Table – CCP
- Data Collection Quality Assessment of a Meal
- Storage Time and Temperature Guidelines
- Pest Control Record

SANITATION REVIEW WITH COMMENTS C-1

Community: _____ **Date:** _____

Evaluator: _____ **Title:** _____

CATEGORY	1	0	COMMENTS
A. FOOD STORAGE			
1. All food is stored in approved clean tightly closed containers			
2. All leftovers properly covered, labeled, dated ≤72 hrs			
3. Cooked food stored above raw in coolers			
4. Food stored off the floor in dry storage & coolers			
5. Floors clear of spilled foods or signs posted			
6. Refrigerator/freezer temps monitored/recorded daily			
7. No signs of rodents or other pests and vermin			
8. Food prep & storage areas are free of exposed pipes above			
9. Cooling units are free of excess moisture or mold			
10. Packages are sealed tight or stored in plastic bins			
Possible poings 10 - SUBTOTAL			
B. ENVIRONMENTAL & SAFETY			
1. Chemicals & cleaning supplies stored in separate room or area			
2. Chemicals & cleaning stored in approved containers, labeled			
3. Brooms, mops, etc stored in separate room or area, off floor			
4. Sheves, cabinets & drawers clean, neat – no knives exposed			
5. Floors dry, clear of spills, signs posted when			

SANITATION REVIEW WITH COMMENTS C-1

CATEGORY	1	0	COMMENTS
needed			
6. Dishware, glasses, pots, pans stored on clean dry surfaces-0 dust			
7. Knives, utensils, flatware stored with handle pointing out			
Possible points 7 – SUBTOTAL			
C. PHYSICAL PLANT & EQUIPMENT			
1. Vents, hoods are free of grease, dust			
2. Filters are free of lint, dust or dirt			
3. Vents, screens, drains are clean & unobstrocted			
4. Dishmachine surfaces free of lime or deposits – nozzles clean			
5. Dishmachine detergent & rinse work properly			
6. Large & small equipment is in good repair			
7. Cutting boards smooth, sanitized before storing			
8. Work surfaces, ceiling clean, shelves no peeling paint or cracks			
9. Walls, floors light fixtures clean			
10. Doors remain closed & are clean			
11. Lighting fixtures are clean, covered, working			
12. All reqired signs posted, clean, legible			
13. Hand sinks clean, liquid soap, paper towels available			
14. No chipping paint, crumbling plaster, loose/missing tiles			
15. Adquate hot water for all needs			
16. Cleaning schedule posted, visible, validated & followed			
Possible points 16 -SUBTOTAL			
D. WASTE DISPOSAL			
1. Garbage conainers non absorbent, no holes, leaks, odors			
2. Garbage containers have tight fitting lids,			

SANITATION REVIEW WITH COMMENTS C-1

CATEGORY	1	0	COMMENTS
kept on at all times			
3. Disposal unit follows loca, state & federal codes. In good repair			
4. Outside dumpster neat, covered, free of vermin, emptied weekly			
E. STAFF HYGIENE			
1. Appropriate attire, hair covering, safe shoes sox/stockings			
2. No signs of contagious illnesses, open sores, coughs, sniffles			
3. Hand washing competency demonstrated or verbalized			
Possible points 3 - SUBTOTAL			
GRAND TOTAL			
TOTAL POSSIBLE POINTS	40	%	

Evaluator Signature:_____

Date _____

FOOD TEMPERATURE COOLING LOG   C-2

Date	Food item	Final cooking	Cooling	Hour 1	Hour 2	Hour 3	Hour 4
		Time/Temp	*Time/Temp*	\multicolumn{4}{c}{Temperature}			

Remember Danger Zone is between $41\,^0F - 140\,^0F$

Cooling tips: remove food item from original container, cut in small pieces, shallow pans, ice bath, freezer, uncover, upper shelf

<u>*Hour 2*</u>: *If temperature is above 70^oF Move to freezer & contact supervisor*

<u>*Hour 4*</u>: *If temperature is above 41^0F call supervisor for corrective actions and/or meal substitution*

*Write all interventions under comments, use cooling tips

CLEANING SCHEDULE ASSIGNMENTS AND PROCEDURES

C-3

Day	Position	Dietary Manager initial weekly. Staff initial daily upon completion of task. **CLEANING TASKS**	Week 1	Week 2	Week 3	Week 4	Week 5
Page 1 of 3		*Dietary Manager: Assign position responsible for each task below*					
AM Aide		Dates					
Sunday		Clean & sanitize food & coffee carts in detail.					
Monday		Clean handwashing sink; check soap and towel supply.					
Tuesday		Wash dishroom floor mats. Sweep back door area. Wash floor mat.					
Wednesday		Clean & organize bottom shelves & lower cabinet in dishroom area.					
Thursday		Clean handwashing sink; check soap and towel supply.					
Friday		Sweep & mop dry storage room. Wipe down ingredient bins.					
Saturday		Clean & organize dish storage areas. Wipe storage area.					
PM Aide		Dates					
Sunday		Clean walls throughout Dietary Department area.					
Monday		Sweep area outside the kitchen. Wash mat.					
Tuesday		Sweep & mop walk-in freezer, refrigerator.					
Wednesday		Detail cleaning of coffee urns, table and storage cabinet.					
Thursday		Clean & sanitize food & coffee carts in detail.					
Friday		Clean hood & filters over stove area.					
Saturday		Wash dishroom floor mats. Sweep back door area. Wash floor mat.					
_____ Aide		Dates					
Sunday		Wipe down beverage carts in detail.					
Monday		Wash trash cans and lids.					
Tuesday		Clean & sanitize ice machine & juice machine.					
Wednesday		Clean & sanitize coffee urn and area, including cabinets.					
Thursday		Wash all trash cans & lids.					
Friday		Clean handwashing sink; check soap and towel supply					
Saturday		Clean doors to outside of Department. Wash assigned walls.					
Page 2 of 3	**ALL Dietary Aides – Daily**	Dates					
		Check & post dishmachine wash & rinse temperatures & record.					
		Leave dishroom area clean, sanitized and organized.					
		Check & post dishmachine sanitizer levels & record.					
		Clean coffee area.					
		Wipe clean all tray delivery carts after each meal.					
Morning Cook		Dates					
Sunday		Clean & organize walk-in refrigerator & freezer shelves.					
Monday		Clean & sanitize mixer, food processor, and other appliances.					
Tuesday		Clean steamer and both toasters thoroughly.					
Wednesday		Clean grease trap, inside of ovens.					

CLEANING SCHEDULE ASSIGNMENTS AND PROCEDURES

C-3

Day	Position	Dietary Manager initial weekly. Staff initial daily upon completion of task. **CLEANING TASKS**	Week 1	Week 2	Week 3	Week 4	Week 5
Thursday		Clean & organize reach-in refrigerator.					
Friday		Clean & sanitize plate warmer.					
Saturday		Clean storage bins, do general cleaning as assigned.					
Evening Cook		**Dates**					
Sunday		Clean & organize reach-in refrigerator.					
Monday		Clean range and microwave thoroughly.					
Tuesday		Clean all walls, stainless steel and counters in cook's preparation area.					
Wednesday		Clean & organize walk-in refrigerator & freezer shelves.					
Thursday		Clean steamtable. Change water in wells.					
Friday		Clean & organize spice cabinets.					
Saturday		Clean grease trap, inside of ovens.					
Page 3 of 3 **All Cooks - Daily** **Dates**							
		✓ Check and post refrigeration temperatures at start of each shift. ✓ Check foods in reach-in refrigerator for labeling, dates. ✓ Clean stoves, ovens & equipment as soon as used. ✓ Always leave work area & floor clean & sanitized at end of shift.					
ALL STAFF - ADDITIONAL CLEANING DUTIES **Dates**							

Evaluator Signature:_____   Date _____

TEMPERATURE RECORDS   C-4

Follow raw meats and casseroles HACCP cooking temperature guidelines at all times. Measure and record all cooked foods temperatures using a clean, calibrated and sanitized probe thermometer prior to serving to ensure doneness.

COOKING TEMPERATURE RECORD

Date/ time	Food	Measure point	Temp. °F	Action taken if temperature too low	Initials

Cooks will record PHF cooked temperatures at the end of cooking and prior to serving. If temperatures do not meet guidelines in recipe or HACCP chart, return to cooking until temperatures are reached. Log corrective action taken, measure and log temperatures again.

Recommended temperatures for hot food
Before serving 135°F or above
During holding 145°F or above

DELIVERIES TEMPERATURE RECORD   C-5

Date	Supplier	Delivery Note #	Vehicle Reg. #	Product Details	Temp	Remarks	Initials

Recommended temperatures for incoming deliveries
Chilled Food 41°F or below
Frozen Food 0°F or below

FREEZER TEMPERATURE RECORD   C-6

Equipment _____   **Month** _____

Week of Date	Monday		Tuesday		Wednesday		Thursday		Initials	Action
	AM	PM	AM	PM	AM	PM	AM	PM		

Week of Date	Friday		Saturday		Sunday		Initials	Action
	AM	PM	AM	PM	AM	PM		

REFRIGERATOR TEMPERATURE RECORD   C-7

Equipment _____   **Month** _____

Week of Date	Monday AM	Monday PM	Tuesday AM	Tuesday PM	Wednesday AM	Wednesday PM	Thursday AM	Thursday PM	Initials		Action

Week of Date	Friday AM	Friday PM	Saturday AM	Saturday PM	Sunday AM	Sunday PM	Initials		Action

COOKING AND COOLING LOG   C-8

Date	Product	Time into cooker	Time out of cooker	Total cook time	Center temp (°F)	Time at start of cooling	Time at end of cooling	Center temp (°F)	Actions taken Y-N	Signature

Note: Ensure that the thermometer probe is clean and sanitized before and after use and calibrated at regular intervals.

POTS AND PANS SANITIZER/TEMPERATURE LOG MONTH/ YEAR   C-9

DATE	BREAKFAST				LUNCH				DINNER				CDM/VENDOR NOTIFIED
	WASH	RINSE	PPM	INITIALS	WASH	RINSE	PPM	INITIALS	WASH	RINSE	PPM	INITIALS	
1													
2													
3													
4													
5													
6													
7													
8													
9													
10													
11													
12													
13													
14													
15													
16													
17													
18													
19													
20													
21													
22													
23													
24													
25													
26													
27													
28													
29													
30													
31													

NOTE: If the sanitizer is < 200PPM notify vendor and supervisor. Use manual sanitzing methods until fixed

CDM REVIEW SIGNATURE:_____   DATE_____

THERMOMETER CALIBRATION RECORD   C-10

Date	Time	Temperature Recorded	Initials	Correction Needed?		Validated Temperature	Initials
				Y	N		

STORAGE LOG   C-11

Refrigerator – Freezer Identification:_____ Month: _____

DATE	Checked by	MET	NOT MET	ACTION
1				
2				
3				
4				
5				
6				
7				
8				
9				
10				
11				
12				
13				
14				
15				
16				
17				
18				
19				
20				
21				
22				
23				
24				
25				
26				
27				
28				
29				
30				
31				

CLEANING SCHEDULE, ASSIGNMENTS & PROCEDURES   C-12

ITEM AREA	WHO	WHEN	WHAT & HOW
Can Opener			Wash handle portion of can opener in dishmachine. Wash the base with a brush and cloth.
Steam Table Counter			Use mild detergent water to clean-rinse well and dry well to prevent streaks and spots. Polish with stainless steel polish.
Coffee Urn Table			Use mild detergent and water to clean. Rinse well and dry thoroughly to prevent streaks and spots. Polish with stainless steel polish.
Food Carts			Using mild germicidal solution (1 oz of bleach to 1 gal of water) and a sponge wipe for the inside and outside of each cart, rinse.
Milk Refrigerator			Shelves and walls should be washed in hot, soapy water to clean. Rinse and dry. Polish exterior with stainless steel polish.
Washing Ticket Holders			Wipe with mild germicidal solution (same mixture as above).
Handwashing Sink			Using a hot detergent water and cleanser, rinse with bleach.
Maintain Condiments			Wipe clean using a mild detergent.
Laundry			Cleaning cloths and aprons washed separate from resident laundry. Properly stored and in good repair.
Dishmachine			After each use with a detergent solution, rinse with fresh water.
Dishwashing Counter			Use hot detergent water with germicidal solution (1 oz of bleach to 1 gal water) and sponge wipe and rinse.
Spice Condiment Shelves			Wash area face with warm detergent solution, use a brush where necessary. Rinse then use dry, clean cloth. Polish.polish.
Cook's Refrigerator			Wash with hot, soapy water. Rinse and dry with clean cloth. Wipe up spilled foods immediately.
Preparation Table			Use mild soap and water to clean. Rinse well and dry thoroughly to prevent streaks immediately.

CLEANING SCHEDULE, ASSIGNMENTS & PROCEDURES   C-12

ITEM AREA	WHO	WHEN	WHAT & HOW
Range			Drip pans should be emptied and washed routinely on a scheduled basis. Boil grates and burners in salt/soda water solution. Clean clogged burner past with a stiff wire brush.
Oven			Use a blunt scraper or wire brush-racks and shelves should be removed and cleaned in a warm detergent solution. Clean oven door and oven after use to remove any food that has spilled before it bakes on.
Defrost Reach-In Refrigerator			Use a mild soap and water to clean. Rinse well - dry thoroughly with a clean cloth.
Grill			Use a pumice stone and clean with vinegar. Scrub until grill is clean. Oil with cooking oil and wipe with a clean cloth.
Blender			Use mild soap and water to clean. Rinse well - dry thoroughly.
Mixer			Wash bowl and a beater with hot detergent water to prevent food from drying on surface.
Kettles/Utensils			Wash both interior and exterior with hot water and detergent. Scour when necessary. Rinse with clean clear water and dry exterior with a clean cloth. Wash in hot water 110°F-120°F with the proper concentration. Water should be changed frequently.
Slicer			Wash with detergent water after use, rinse and dry it with a clean cloth.
Toaster			Disconnect cord from electrical outlet - remove and wash the toast guide and crumb tray with detergent water.
Garbage Disposal			Use warm detergent solution with germicide and a sponge for cleaning.
Ice Cream Refrigerator			Use a mild detergent water to clean - rinse well and dry thoroughly to prevent streaks and spotting.
Cleaning Closet			After each use, all equipment should be cleaned and rinsed before storage. Mops must be washed, rinsed and rung out and allowed to air dry before returning to the closet. Use detergent and hot water.

CLEANING SCHEDULE, ASSIGNMENTS & PROCEDURES   C-12

ITEM AREA	WHO	WHEN	WHAT & HOW
Floor Mats			Remove from kitchen. Take outside and scrub with hot water and germicidal solution.
Floors			Floors must be washed daily: Use detergent and hot water - dry thoroughly.
Floor Drains			Covered, cleaned and free of odors.
Trash Barrels			Each time the garbage is emptied, pour in one gallon of hot detergent solution into the can. Scrub with a long-handled stiff brush.
Trash Area			Swept and mopped routinely.
Stainless Steel Counters			Use mild detergent water to clean. Rinse well and dry thoroughly to prevent streaking and spots. Polish with stainless steel polish.
Storeroom Floor			Floor should be washed in storeroom using detergent hot water and detergent. Dry thoroughly.
Stock Away			Merchandise should be put away as soon as possible after delivery is made.
Hoods			Clean inside and out. Wash hood with detergent solution using brush, sponge or cloth.
Ceilings			Use a mild detergent with germicidal solution and wipe clean with sponge.
Walls			Painted walls and ceiling should be washed with a mild detergent solution, rinse using a clean cloth and dried to eliminate streaking.

Date_____   Evaluator:_____

PRE-MEAL CHECKLIST   C-13

This is a quality assurance tool to be completed 15-30 minutes prior to the start of EVERY meal. More than one taste- tester is recommended. One to two ounces of EVERY FOOD and EVER Consistency is put on a plate by the cook for sampling. The sampling is done in an out of the way location in the kitchen by all dietary staff using a separate eating utensil per taste per person to prevent cross-contamination.
If the answer is no, then immediate action needs to be taken.

DATE:_____ MEAL:_____

1. Are the steam tables on and hot?
2. Are the plate heaters on and are the plates hot? 120-160 degrees?
3. Are the pellets hot? 220 degrees?
4. Have Food Temperatures beenTaken?
5. Is the milk cold?
6. Has coffee been made?
7. Is the coffee at or below 145°F for safety?
8. Hairnets & aprons worn?
9. Gloves available?
10. Utensils are correct with spreadsheets?
11. Cold Food pulled?
12. Cold Beverages pulled?
13. Condiments stocked?
14. Condiments for this meal? Crackers, mayo, lemon juice, vinegar?
15. Garnishes prepared / pulled?
16. Are the tray carts clean? Inside? __ Outside? __Wheels? __

Spreadsheets reviewed by:
(insert your initials below)

STARTER _____
SERVER/COOK _____
CHECKER/LOADER _____
CARTS _____

Food item	Temp. >160°f and >165°f leftovers	Utensil- indicate serving size and utensil used	How does the food look? Color, texture	How does the food taste? ✓ Excellent ✓ Ok ✓ Not good	Recommendations

DAILY KITCHEN CLEANING SCHEDULE C-14

Cleaning Job	Position	Shift	WEEK 1 date:							WEEK 2 date:							WEEK 3 date:							WEEK 4 date:						
			M	T	W	Th	F	S	Su	M	T	W	Th	F	S	Su	M	T	W	Th	F	S	Su	M	T	W	Th	F	S	Su
Counters		am																												
		pm																												
Floors		am																												
		pm																												
Food Carts		am																												
		pm																												
Utility Carts		am																												
		pm																												
Steam Table		am																												
		pm																												
Can Opener		am																												
		pm																												
Slicer		am																												
		pm																												
Mixer		am																												
		pm																												
Toaster		am																												
		pm																												
Coffee Machine		am																												
		pm																												
Dish Machine		am																												
		pm																												
Steamer		am																												
		pm																												
Freezer Label/Date		pm																												
		pm																												

Initial appropriate box when task completed

WEEKLY CLEANING SCHEDULE January to June   C-15

Year:_____ January to June

Cleaning Job	By	Shift	January				February				March				April				May				June			
			Wk 1	Wk 2	Wk 3	Wk 4	Wk 1	Wk 2	Wk 3	Wk 4	Wk 1	Wk 2	Wk 3	Wk 4	Wk 1	Wk 2	Wk 3	Wk 4	Wk 1	Wk 2	Wk 3	Wk 4	Wk 1	Wk 2	Wk 3	Wk 4
Refrigerators		Date																								
		Init																								
Freezers		Date																								
		Init																								
Store Room		Date																								
		Init																								
Stove		Date																								
		Init																								
Ovens		Date																								
		Init																								
Hand Sink		Date																								
		Init																								
Shelves		Date																								
		Init																								
Food Warmer		Date																								
		Init																								

Initial appropriate box when tast completed

MONTHLY CLEANING SCHEDULE - July to December   C-16

Year:_____ July to December

Cleaning Job	By	Shift	January				February				March				April				May				June			
			Wk 1	Wk 2	Wk 3	Wk 4	Wk 1	Wk 2	Wk 3	Wk 4	Wk 1	Wk 2	Wk 3	Wk 4	Wk 1	Wk 2	Wk 3	Wk 4	Wk 1	Wk 2	Wk 3	Wk 4	Wk 1	Wk 2	Wk 3	Wk 4
Refrigerators		Date																								
		Init																								
Freezers		Date																								
		Init																								
Store Room		Date																								
		Init																								
Stove		Date																								
		Init																								
Ovens		Date																								
		Init																								
Hand Sink		Date																								
		Init																								
Shelves		Date																								
		Init																								
Food Warmer		Date																								
		Init																								

Intial appropriate box when tast completed

MONTHLY CLEANING SCHEDULE   C-17

Year: _____

Cleaning Job	By	Date & Initial	Jan	Feb	Mar	Apr	May	Jun	Jul	Aug	Sep	Oct	Nov	Dec
Trashcans		Date												
		Initial												
Drawers		Date												
		Initial												
Fryer		Date												
		Initial												
Emergency Supplies Inspect and or Rotate		Date												
		Initial												

Initial appropriate box when tast completed

PRODUCTION SCHEDULES AND STANDARDS - HACCP BASED INSTRUCTIONS C-18

A. Schedule and timing

1. Basic thawing and pre-preparation instructions will be included in the production schedule.
2. Check timetable for preparation on recipe and consider recipe timing when planning.
3. Time preparation to finish all food as close as possible to serving time, allowing for preparation of texture altered foods.

B. Produce
1. Wash all fruits and vegetables in cold running water before using.
2. Use only vegetables in good condition. Remove wilted or deteriorated leaves of greens.
3. Add dressing to salad prior to serving or keep refrigerated.
4. Store prepared fruits and vegetables in refrigerator following correct storage procedures.
5. Wash all melons in room temperature water and scrub with vegetable brush to clean skin before cutting or peeling.

C. Meats and Poultry
1. Cook most meats at a low temperature to retain flavor and tenderness.
2. Season meat lightly. Do not salt ham.
3. Make sure frozen meat is thoroughly defrosted before cooking unless it is individually quick frozen (IQF) and does not require thawing or recipe states otherwise.
4. Wash all poultry before cooking.
5. Maintain a temperature chart when temperature reaches 145°F until processing is completed and product is incorporated into the recipe.
6. Cooking process must heat ingredients to 165°F for food safety.
7. It is safer to use boned poultry when using it for this purpose.
8. Use meat thermometer to determine internal temperature of all meat and poultry. Do not serve undercooked meats.

PRODUCTION SCHEDULES AND STANDARDS - HACCP BASED INSTRUCTIONS C-18

D. Eggs

1. Use only pasteurized eggs.
2. Hot hard-cooked eggs may be left at room temperature if to be served within the hour (2 hour Food Safety HACCP Rule).
3. Do not mix batches of freshly prepared eggs with eggs in the steam table.
   Example: When serving scrambled eggs, do not add a new batch of freshly cooked - use a clean pan.
4. Well cooked eggs have both white and yolk firm.
5. Raw eggs and foods containing raw eggs should be cooked to minimum internal temperature of 140°F for 3½ minutes (yolk and white are set).
6. Eggs and egg-rich foods should not be out of the refrigerator for more than two hours, including serving time (Food Safety HACCP Rule).
7. Do not pool eggs.
8. The following cooking times are now recommended by Cornell University, the American Egg Board, and the Egg Nutrition Center.
   - Scrambled - 1 minute at a cooking surface temperature of 250°F.
   - Poached - 5 minutes in boiling water.
   - Sunnyside - 7 minutes at a cooking surface temperature of 250°F on one side, then turn the egg and fry another 2 minutes on the other side.
   - Hard Cooked - 7 minutes in boiling water

HAZARD ANALYSIS PROCESS   C-19

PROCESS STEP_____   Date: _____

1. Hazard Analysis Table   Product: _____

Processing Step	Potential Hazards C = Chemical P = Physical B = Biological	Is this potential food safety hazard significant?	Justification of decision	Preventive Measures Recommended	Is this step a CCP? + = yes 0 = no

Facility: _____   **Evaluator**: _____

HACCP PLAN SUMMARY   C-20

Date:

ROP CCP HACCP PLAN   **Product:** _____

Critical Control Point (CCP)	Hazard Type	Critical Limits	Monitoring				Corrective Action	Verification Activities	Record Keeping Procedures
			What	How	How Often	Who			

Facility: _____

Evaluator: _____

STORAGE TIME AND TEMPERATURE GUIDELINES C-21

Dairy	Refrigerator 35°F – 40°F	Freezer 0°F
Non-dairy Liquid Creamer	3 weeks	See package
Cream or Half & half unopened	3 weeks	Not recommended
Cream or Half & half opened	1 week	Not recommended
Cream, heavy, whipping	1 week	Not recommended
Margarine	3 months	1 year
Evaporated milk opened	1 week	Not Recommended
Whole milk	1 week or see expiration date	1 month
Non-fat dry reconstituted	1 week	1 month

Eggs	Refrigerator 35°F – 40°F	Freezer 0°F
Eggs fresh in shell	2 to 5 weeks	Not recommended
Eggs fresh out of shell whipped	1 day	1 month
Home prepared puddings	1 week	1 week – may thaw lumpy

Fruits	Refrigerator 35°F – 40°F	Freezer 0°F
Canned fruits in syrup or juice	1 week	2 months (thaws mushy)
Juices canned or bottled	2 weeks	In glass or plastic up to 1 year

Meats, Poultry, Fish	Refrigerator 35°F – 40°F	Freezer 0°F
Beef	5 to 7 days	6 to 12 months
Veal and Pork	5 to 7 days	4 to 8 months
Lamb	5 to 7 days	6 to 9 months
Chicken and Turkey	2 days	9 to 12 months
Sausages	2 to 4 days	2 to 4 months
Cooked meats & meat dishes	5 to 7 days	3 to 4 months
Meat gravies and broths	5 to 7 days	3 to 4 months
Bacon	7 days	1 to 2 months
Ham	7 days	1 to 2 months
Canned tuna in water, opened	5 days	1 month
Fish fresh or frozen (thawed)	3 to 5 days	4 to 6 months
Fish cooked	5 to 7 days	Not recommended

Miscellaneous	Refrigerator 35°F – 40°F	Freezer 0°F
Vegetables, fresh	5 to 7 days	8 to 9 months
Potatoes, fresh	30 days	Not recommended
Rice, cooked	5 to 7 days	1 month (thaws mushy)
Soups and Stews	2 to 3 days	5 to 6 months
Sandwiches	2 to 3 days	1 month
Casseroles	2 to 3 days	1 month

QUALITY ASSESSMENT OF A MEAL   C-22

COMMUNITY: _____ **DATE:** _____ **EVALUATOR:** _____

MEAL CHECKED *(attach copy of menu)* _____ **DIET CHECKED:** _____

TEMPERATURE	HOT FOOD					COLD FOOD			
Menu Item	Soup	Entree	Starch	Vegetable	Beverage	Sandwich	Leafy Salad	Dessert *(dairy based)*	Beverage *(milk & dairy)*

1. At TRAY LINE
    Standard Temperature
    Actual Temperature
	170 °F	160 °F	160 °F	160 °F	170 °F	41 °F	Cool/ Crisp	Cool*/ 41 °F	41 °F

2. At TRAY-LINE POINT OF SERVICE
    Standard
    Actual/Test tray
	165°F
	145°F
		165 °F
		145°F
			145 °F
			140 °F
				145 °F
				140 °F
					145 °F
					150 °F
						41 °F
						45 °F
							41°f
							Cool/ Crisp
								41 °F	41 °F

Temperature Standard: hot breads @ 100 °F to 120 °F; sliced bread, cookies, cakes @ room temperature; potentially hazardous salads & desserts @ 41 °F; other salads & desserts cool, crisp, 45 °F to 50 °F.

3. TIMING: Record the time for each activity listed below					d. Cart left kitchen				
a. Time at which tray line temperature recorded					e. Cart arrived in dining area				
b. Steam table loaded					f. Tray distribution started				
c. Tray line service started					g. Tray distribution ended				

ASSESSMENT OF MEAL SERVICE:
Indicate condition for items 4 through 10 below as S for satisfactory and NI for needs improvement.

FOOD ASSESSMENT	Soup	Entree	Starch	Vegetable	Beverage	Sandwich	Salad	Dessert	Beverage
4. PORTION SIZE									
5. APPERANCE OF FOOD									
6. GARNISHES & PRESENTATION									
7. TASTE AND AROMA									
8. ALL MENU ITEMS SERVED									
TRAY ASSESSMENT	Tray	Napkin	Flat ware	Glass ware	Dishes	Delivery System		Heat Keeping System	
9. NO MISSING ITEMS									
10. CORRECT SET-UP									
11. ALL FOOD COVERED	YES	NO							
12. OVERALL QUALITY OF THE MEAL	*EXCELLENT*		*VERY GOOD*		*GOOD*		*FAIR*		*POOR*

CORRECTIVE ACTION NEEDED: ___NO ___YES *If yes, attach Action Plan for correction to this evaluation.*

PEST CONTROL MONITORING RECORD   C-23

Date	Area	Signs of infestation	Action taken	Signature

To be completed by the DM monthly or whenever pests are noted & filed

FOOD SANITATION & SAFETY D

PURPOSE

The incidence of foodborne illness outbreaks has increased in the past decade. Cross-contamination due to careless handling and unsafe food temperature contribute to a significant number of foodborne illnesses. The incidence of food-temperature deficiencies continues to be high throughout the nation. Food handlers are the single most common source of food contamination leading to foodborne illnesses in healthcare facilities. Safe food handling techniques will help reduce the incidence of foodborne illness. It is the responsibility of every staff member to follow the safe food handling gidelines to help prevent the spread of infection and illness and ensure regulatory compliance and resident safety.

FOOD FROM OUTSIDE SOURCES D-1

PURPOSE

To ensure residents whishing to eat food from other sources, such as home or restaurants, are able to do so safely.

PROCEDURE

    A. Temperature Control for Safety (TCS) foods
      1. Foods brought in must be in a safe container
         a. in original bottle with label intact
         b. in spill-proof covered container dated and labeled properly
         c. in a resealable container with original label, or if transferred to another container correctly labeled and dated

      2. Label food brought in with name of resident, item, and date brought to facility and use by or discard date and stored in a designated refrigerator apart from the facility food.

      3. Service of foods brought in
         a. Items such as salad dressings, favorite creamers, favorite jams or spreads, ice cream, sherbet or sorbet can be served directly from the bottle/jar to the residents plate or placed at the table for resident's exclusive use
         b. Items that need to be re-heated are transferred into a microwave-safe container and heated to an internal temperature of 165°F and served.
         c. Items such as fruit, deli meats or spreads, cheese are portioned out and served on a plate.
         d. Items such as fresh produce must be rinsed well under running water prior to service to residents.
      4. Retention of foods
         a. Condiment type foods may be kept for 2 months/60 days or according to the manufacturer expiration date
         b. Protein containing foods such casserole, beef stew and soup may be kept for 3 days
         c. Lunchmeat and cheeses may be kept for 7 days

    B. Non-TCS Foods
      1. Foods brought in must be in a sealed air-tight container to prevent staleness and to reduce chances of vermin.
      2. Container must be labeled with the resident's name, date and content.
      3. Container may be kept in resident's room.

FOOD FROM OUTSIDE SOURCES   D-1

   C. Food from a restaurant—*"Take Out"*
1. For immediate consumption the food can be eaten whenever the resident wishes. If the food has cooled, it can be reheated in the microwave. Caution should be used to not overheat and cause burns.
2. For *"doggie bags"*-the food would be treated the same way as a TCS food. It must not be left at room temperature for more than 2 hours.

   D. Education should include but is not limited to
1. Letters to families regarding safe food handling and the need for labeling and dating foods
2. Inservice education for staff on receiving, storage, and disposal of foods
3. Discussion at family meetings and/or care plan meetings as warranted
4. Document all education provided in the appropriate forms and format

HACCP MANAGEMENT   D-2

I. HACCP REVIEW: Managing Food Hazard Analysis Critical Control Point

1. Causes of Foodborne Illness.
   - Single most common leading source of food contamination leading to foodborne illnesses.
   - Foodborne illness can be reduced by determining potentially hazardous and practicing safe food handling techniques.

2. Definition of HACCP.
   - An acronym that stands for *hazard analysis critical control point.*
   - *Hazard analysis:* is the process of identifying and evaluating potential hazards associated with foods during preparation.
   - *Control points:* are developed to prevent or control contamination or increased hazard.
       a. Each recipe is analyzed for times during which bacterial growth may occur due to adverse reactions.
       b. These periods of time are called **critical control points.**

3. Plan Description.
   - A *HAACP* plan is a document describing the procedures used in a specific facility to prepare Time/Temperature Control for Safety Foods (TCS).
   - It is based on a general plan that provides basic guidelines.

4. Purpose.
   - Focus on the flow of food from receiving to service.
   - Increase customer confidence of food safety.
   - Meet regulatory requirement: County, State, Federal.

5. Considerations: The following must be considered when developing a facility specific HACCP plan: **Menu, Equipment, Process, Flow, Staffing.**

6. Basic Principles: *There are seven basic principles/steps that must be considered when developing a HACCP program.*
   I. **Steps one, two and three assist in developing the system**.

HACCP MANAGEMENT D-2

Step 1: Identify TCS in recipes and describe preventative measures.
Implementation: Identify Time/Temperature Control for Safety Foods in recipes and describe preventive measures.
- Determine where and when to prevent problems by looking at the flow of food in your kitchen and identifying potential areas and times during which contamination may occur.

Step 2: Identify all the critical control points (CCP) in the process and establish a flow chart.
Implementation:
- Check recipes to identify all potential problem "points".
- Find the essential points to prevent or reduce the hazard.
- Design a flow chart of the stages and processes each type of food takes from delivery to distribution.
- The last point during which the hazard can be controlled is a *critical control point (CCP)*.

Step 3: Establish standards that must be met at each critical control point.
Implementation:
- Set limits to control problems.
- Establish temperature checks for food during the "flow" process.
- Set standards that must be met for food to be considered safe.

II. *Four and five enable implementation of the system.*
Step 4: Monitor critical control points and determine whether criteria is being met.
Implementation:
- Focus on critical points of time and temperature controls.
- Establish procedures to identify control problems.

Step 5: Establish corrective actions to correct the hazard immediately.
Implementation:
- Decide what to do if the critical limits are not met and include the plan.
- Write out plan and instruct staff.
- Incorporate plan in recipes.
- Develop and post flow charts for specific TCS groups.
-

III. *Six and seven help maintain the system and ensure its effectiveness.*
Step 6: Set-up an effective record keeping procedure that documents the HACCP system.
Implementation:
- Use a QA&A study data collection form.

HACCP MANAGEMENT   D-2

- Set up a record-keeping system, and make routine reviews of all records.
- Determine which forms are needed.
- Determine filing location.
- Determine where to post /place flow charts.

Step 7: Establish procedures for verification that the HACCP system is working correctly.
Implementation:
- Set up a department meeting time to review collected data.
- Discuss procedures that need retraining review, monitoring, etc.
- Involve interdisciplinary team members as needed.
- Conduct periodic audits to ensure that the HACCP system in working correctly.
- Determine frequency of audits.
- Assign staff to conduct audits.

SAMPLE FLOW CHART

Establish check points

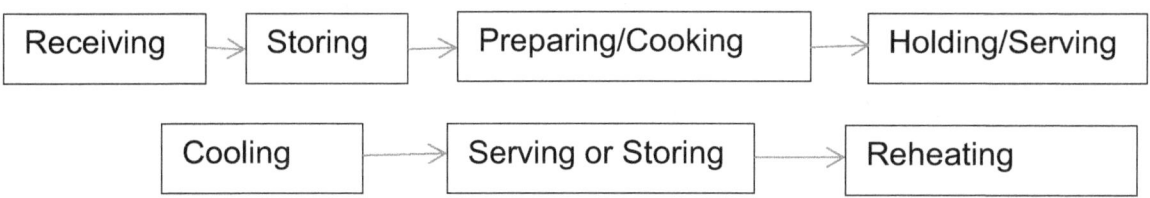

HACCP MANAGEMENT   D-2

TRAINING

    a. Assess training needs
    b. Establish Objectives
    c. Plan and develop training program.
    d. Identify appropriate trainers
    e. Choose appropriate materials.
    f. Choose appropriate materials.
    g. Establish a location for the training.
    h. Select convenient training time/date.
    i. Plan incentives for completing training.
    j. Evaluate effectiveness of training.

TRAINING TOOLS

    1. Written materials.
    2. Audio visual materials.
    3. Handouts.
    4. Posters – reminders.
    5. Lecture, presentation.
    6. Demonstrations.
    7. Hands-on
    8. Audience Feed back

MONITORING

    A. Temperature Records.
    B. Recipes
    C. Observation.
    D. QAPI

TEMPERATURE GUIDELINES   D-3

Cook foods to proper temperature

Foods are safely cooked when they are heated at a high enough temperature for a long enough time to kill disease causing organisms. The target temperature is different for different foods. Make sure that each food is cooked to the recommended temperature which ranges from 145° Fahrenheit (63° Celsius) to 165° Fahrenheit (74° Celsius).

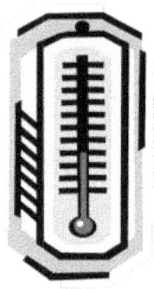

Cool foods promptly at proper temperature

Once food is prepared it should be eaten right away. Since cool temperatures slow the growth of bacteria, if you're saving it for later, cool in the refrigerator to 41° degrees Fahrenheit (5° Celsius).

Proper thawing and reheating temperature

Thaw all frozen foods in the refrigerator and not at room temperature to avoid spoilage. When reheating be sure that the inside of the food reaches 165° Fahrenheit (74° Celsius) to be safe.

SAFE USE OF GLOVES   D-4

Safe food-handling practices in the dining services Services department is serious business, and it is the responsibility of every dining services staff member to ensure that all aspects of food-preparation are accomplished using the best safety practices possible.

PURPOSE OF WEARING GLOVES WHEN HANDLING FOOD

The purpose of wearing gloves when handling food is three-fold:
1. Protect Dining services Service worker from the following:
   ◊ harsh chemicals
   ◊ hot temperatures
   ◊ contamination from raw or unwashed foods (raw meat, raw vegetables)
   ◊ cross-contamination (cleaning soiled areas/items, washing dishes, removing trash)
2. Protect food from contamination
3. Protect residents from foodborne illnesses

SIMPLE RULES
The following simple rules will serve as a guide for the use of wearing gloves in the Dining services Services department.
- *Don't* use your bare hand(s) to serve food; if hand(s) must be used, wear clean, disposable gloves.
- *Don't* pick or scratch at parts of your body:
   ◊ nose
   ◊ ears
   ◊ head
   ◊ hair
   ◊ other
- *Don't* touch a pimple or sore.
- *Don't* cough or sneeze without protecting the food; instead, you should do the following:
   ◊ Cover your nose and mouth.
   ◊ Move away from food and equipment.
   ◊ Wash your hands immediately after sneezing or coughing.
- *Don't* wash hands in food-preparation sinks; use designated hand-washing sinks.
- *Don't* smoke in areas where contamination could easily occur:
   ◊ near food
   ◊ in food-preparation areas

SAFE USE OF GLOVES   D-4

- ◊ in serving areas
- *Don't* pick up food with your bare hands:
  - ◊ bread
  - ◊ ice
  - ◊ garnishes
  - ◊ other foods
- *Don't* touch eating areas of eating and drinking implements:
  - ◊ flatware
  - ◊ straws
  - ◊ food area of plates
  - ◊ glasses and cups
    - rim
    - inside
- *Don't* handle place settings after wiping tables or bussing soiled dishes.
- *Don't* taste food with cooking spoons or with fingers; use a clean spoon each time.
- *Don't* lick your fingers.
- *Don't* drink and handle personal drinking cups while working without washing your hands immediately afterward.
- *Don't* wear soiled gloves.
- *Don't* handle chemicals *without* wearing protective gloves.
- *Don't* immerse your hands in hot water *without* wearing protective gloves.

SAFE USE OF GLOVES   D-4

USE OF GLOVES

Gloves help create a barrier between hands and food, preventing cross contamination of foods. Proper handwashing and food handling techniques must still be emphasized and used to prevent accidental contamination due to inappropriate gloved hands use.

Gloves worn during food preparation will protect hands, however, inappropriate use of gloves will cause cross contamination and increase the possibility of foodborne illness, food contamination and food spoilage. Following a few simple rules will ensure that foodservice workers do not misuse gloved hands.

Follow these simple rules when using gloves:
1. Never use gloves in place of handwashing.
◊ Always wash hands prior to wearing a fresh pair of gloves.
◊ Discard gloves once used – do not rewash and reuse.
2. Change gloves as soon as necessary:
◊ When soiled or torn
◊ Before changing tasks or work location
◊ Every few hours if worn continuously
◊ Whenever hands sweat excessively (then wash hands prior to replacing gloves)
◊ After handling raw meat
◊ Prior to handling foods that will not be cooked or heated again

COMMON CAUSES OF FOODBORNE ILLNESS   D-5

FOOD SAFETY REGULATIONS

Food safety regulations and guidelines are developed and enforced at 3 levels, federal, state and county. The agencies in charge of food safety regulate the food industry from initial production until it reaches the customers' plate. Their main role is to oversee the entire food production systems and protect the food we eat.

The Dietary Manager (DM) is responsible for maintaining standards of food sanitation by ensuring that time and temperature control requirements are followed

- A. State and local regulations are under the jurisdiction of government agencies under either environmental health, public health or the department of agriculture.

- B. In order to assess compliance with regulations periodic inspections and audits are conducted by these agencies. Often past compliance history will influence frequency of inspections.

- C. Federal agencies responsible for ensuring the safety of our food supply include Food and Drug Administration (FDA), US Department of Agriculture (USDA), Centers for Disease Control and Prevention (CDC). Others such as the US Department of Commerce (USDC and the Environmental Protection Agency (EPA) have specific jurisdiction over select areas.

- D. The Centers for Disiease Control (CDC) responsibility is to protect public health therough the prevention and control of diseases

- E. The Occupational Safety and Health Administration (OSHA), created by the Department of Labor to enforce the Occupational Safety and Health Act, protects empolyees through estalished health stadards and regulations on safety, noise and other working conditions. Their primary duties are not to protect the general public but to protect employees by enforcing health and safety regulations in the workplace.

- F. Several laws were also in eacted in the effort to protect our food sources.

COMMON CAUSES OF FOODBORNE ILLNESS   D-5

These include the Food, Drug and Cosmetic Act, Federal Meat Inspection Act, Federal Poultry Products Inspection Act, Eggs Products Inspection Act and Nutrition Labeling and Eduction Act.

G. The FDA also designated some substances as "Generally Recognized As Safe", now known as GRAS. The term describes additives that are used in foods that have been demonstrated as being safe for the consumer.

Although the names and responsibilities of these agencies have changed since their inception for the most part their primary roles have remained the same; to develop and approve the regulation, inform the food industry and the public, enforce compliance and encourage the food industry to comply and educate the public.

FOOD SAFETY AND SANITATION MANAGEMENT

Foodborne illness affects millions of people annually and is believed to cause at least 5000 deaths each year and cost the food industry and employers billions of dollars a year. Moreover, foodborne illness may result in lengthy and legal repercussions and be very costly.

HAZARDS TO FOOD SAFETY

Bacteria are the most common cause of foodborne illness in food establishments. Some bacteria can produce spores to help them survive when conditions are cold, hot and dry. Spores are dangerous because they ca survive cooking. The best way to control bacteria is to

1. Keep foods out of the temperature danger zone
2. Prevent contamination and cross-contamination of foods
3. Pratice good personal hygiene
4. Keep in mind the 3 main **hazards to food safety**
   a. **Infection** caused by eating food that contains living disease-causing microorganisms.
   b. **Intoxication** caused by eating food that contains a harmful chemical or toxin produced by bacteria or other sources.
   c. **Toxin-mediated infection** caused by eating a food that contains harmful microorganisms that will produce a toxin once inside the human body.

COMMON CAUSES OF FOODBORNE ILLNESS D-5

Viruses

Viruses are different from bacteria and yet cause illness. They are smaller in size than bacteria, require a living host to grow, do not grow in foods and need only a few particles to cause infection.

Parasites

Parasites are small or microscopic in size and need a host in which to live and survive. Parasitic infection is far less common than other bacterial or viral foodborne illness or infection.

Chemicals

Chemical hazards are either man-made or occurring naturally. It is important to buy food from approved sources and avoid direct contact with chemicals and poisons or some specific metals.

Allergens

Food allergies are not uncommon and vary in severity from a mild gastrointestinal illness to anaphylactic shock. The most common foods causing allergic reactions are shellfish, milk, egg, wheat, peanuts, soy, tree nuts and fish.

Time and Temperature Abuse
- Temperature abuse occurs when foods are held at temperatures that permit the growwth of harmful microorganisms. It is commonly caused by insufficiently cooked food or food that is cooked in a way as to allow harmful microorganisms to survive.
- Temperature Danger Zone: 41°F to 140°F (5°C to 60°C)
- Super Danger Zone: 70°F to 140°F (21°C to 49°C)

FOOD TEMPERATURE SAFETY   D-6

SAFETY TIPS

"Hot foods" are intended to be served hot and, when being held on a steam table, are to be kept hot enough to prevent bacteria from growing and increasing the likelihood of a foodborne illness outbreak. The preparation of "hot foods" includes safe food-handling techniques that will prevent such an outbreak.

- Allow adequate time to thaw and cook frozen foods:
  - Follow thawing instructions for specific foods.
  - Often, it takes up to twice as long to cook frozen foods.
- Temperatures for preparing hot foods:
  - 160°F to 212°F, using one of several cooking processes
    - boiling
    - simmering
    - baking
    - frying
    - sautéing
    - roasting
  - above 160°F for 15 seconds kills most food-poisoning bacteria
- Cook foods thoroughly:
  - Cook meat and poultry according to temperatures in standardized recipes.
  - Use a meat thermometer:
    - For roasts, boned or boneless: Insert the tip of the thermometer into the thickest part of the meat, avoiding fat or bone.
    - For poultry, insert the tip of the thermometer into the thickest part of the thigh, next to the body.
- Do not interrupt the cooking process:
  - Cook meat and poultry completely during one cooking interval.
  - Partial cooking encourages bacterial growth before cooking is complete.
    (Refer to meat cooking temperature chart below)
- Holding hot foods:
  - Holding temperatures: 135 °F to 160°F
  - should not be held more than two hours

    Note: Once out of heat source, food quickly drops to the danger zone (between 39°F to 140°F) in which bacteria thrive.

  - steam tables and chafing dishes
    - designed to maintain holding temperatures

FOOD TEMPERATURE SAFETY   D-6

- limitations
    - do not always keep foods sufficiently hot
    - may not keep foods heated evenly or thoroughly
    - should never be used to reheat food
- Food Danger Zone:
    ◊ Bacteria grows best within the temperature danger zone of between 41 °F to 140 °F (or exactly 42 °F and 139 °F). The most rapid growth occurs at the ideal range of 70 °F to 120 °F. It is imperative that cooking, cooling, and reheating processes are designed to move foods rapidly through the ideal range (70 °F to 120 °F). Whether cooking, cooling or reheating, plan to reach and exceed temperatures between 70 °F to 120 °F in two hours or less.

Minimum Safe Internal Cooking Temperatures
All temperatures are for a minimum of 15 seconds unless specified

Food Item	Internal Temperature
Poultry, stuffing, stuffed meats, stuffed pasta, casseroles	165 °F
Pork, ham, bacon, cured meats, precooked meats	145 °F
Ground meats, sausage	155 °F
Beef and pork roast meats	145 °F *for 3 minutes*
Steaks, patties, all types	145 °F
Fish	145 °F
Fresh eggs (shell eggs)	145 °F
PHF cooked in microwave	165 °F – *stand 2 minutes after*

SAFETY TIPS
The following safety tips for perishables will be an aid for you as you prepare and store cold foods:

- Delivery:
    ◊ Store perishable foods before dry and other non-perishables.
    ◊ Do not leave perishable foods on a loading dock or at room temperature.
- Refrigeration:
    ◊ Repeated handling increases the possibility of introducing harmful bacteria, especially to meat and poultry.

FOOD TEMPERATURE SAFETY   D-6

- ◊ Leave products in the product wrapper, unless it is torn or otherwise damaged.
- ◊ If the product wrapper is torn, rewrap the product in plastic or aluminum foil and seal tightly to prevent moisture loss. If product is rewrapped it must be labeled with contents and date.
- ◊ Rotate stock, using first in, first out (FIFO).
- ◊ Do not keep foods past storage guidelines.

- Freezing:
  - ◊ Some frozen meats may exhibit freezer burn (white, dried-out patches on the surface of meat). Freezer burn is not harmful, but does affect taste and quality.
    - will not cause illness
    - makes meat tough and tasteless
    - avoid, by wrapping items appropriately:
      - heavy freezer paper
      - heavy plastic wrap
      - aluminum foil
  - ◊ stock rotation
    - Use FIFO system.
    - Date freezer packages.

- Thawing
  - ◊ Never thaw meat and poultry at room temperature; bacteria grow rapidly at room temperature.
  - ◊ The following guidelines will ensure safety of thawed food items and decrease opportunities for bacterial growth:
    - in the refrigerator at 41 °F until thawed
    - cooking above 135 °F - refer to meats cooking time guidelines
    - under running water at 70 °F for no more than 2 hours in a clean container, unwrapped, allowing water flow to remove blood and other particles that come lose
    - In microwave if part of the cooking process; food made be transferred to oven, pot, skillet, grill or steamer and heated to at least 135 °F (check state regulations).

- Storing leftovers
  - ◊ Never cool leftovers at room temperature.
  - ◊ Follow proper procedure for cooling leftovers or pre-prepared foods. The following cooling process will ensure food safety and decrease opportunities for bacterial growth

FOOD TEMPERATURE SAFETY   D-6

- Place food in shallow pans (2 in. deep) in the refrigerator or freezer.
- Divide foods into small containers or portions.
- Divide large meats into smaller pieces.
- Use ice baths to cool down rapidly.
- Protect food from spills and cross contamination.
- Do not cover during the cooling process until food is below 41°F.
- Check and record temperature during the cooling process to ensure it cools down from 70 °F to 41°F or below within four hours.
- "Ice baths" may be used to drop food temperature to below 41°F.
- Discard food that does not cool to 41°F within four hours.

What Makes Food Unsafe?

Although most food is safe it's important to recognize the factors that can potentially make foods unsafe. The foods most likely to become unsafe contain moisture, protein, and a netural or slightly acidic pH. When these foods remain at room temperature for a lenghty period of time their naturally occuring bacteria grows and can cause illness. Controlling the growth of bacteria in foods is called *time and temperature control*.

Time and Temperature Control

These foods are known to require proper temperature control during storage, cooking, holding and serving. Keep refrigerated

Milk, dairy & other milk products	Eggs except pasteurized
Shellfish, crustacea	Fish
Baked Potatoes	Sliced melons
Textured soy protein in meat alternatives	Meat, beef, ork, lamb
Raw sprouts and seeds	Heat treated plant food: rice, legumes, vegetables
Poultry	Untreaed garlic & oil mixtures

In addition to time and temperature control there are external contaminants that can make foods unsafe..

- Biological hazards: viruses, parasites, fungi, some plants, mushroom & seafood
- Chemical hazards: pesticides, food additives, preservatives, cleaning supplies & toxic metals leaching from cookware or equipment
- Physical hazards: foreign objects falling into foods that are undetected or bones & grizzle

COMPETENCE VALIDATION   E

WORKING HEALTHY, WORKING SAFELY

This book is written as a convenient, consolidated guide to assist dining services staff in basic cleaning and sanitizing of kitchen equipment physical plant. The instructions are not intended for maintenance supervisors or to replace manufacturer instructions and manuals.

Competence is defined as the ability to do something successfully and/or efficiently. Competencies in this section are intended for the readers to test their own skills and undertanding of these procedures. The questions are broken down into specific skills or tasks, described in terms of what specific behavior are required at different levels of proficiency. To demonstrate competence in a particular job or task, a person is expected to perform tasks directly related to the job at a target proficiency level.

There are two quizzes, one for sanitation and food safety and one for employee safety. After the two qizzes the competence observations are a useful method for supervisory staff to determine if further employee training is needed.

The quizzes in this section are intended to help those reading the cleaning procedures determine whether they have learned the basis skills to complete each task for the areas and/or equipment described efficiently and safely. As the author and consultant registered dietitian nutritionist I recommend using this book to provide training on how to clean, and suggest keeping it accessible as a reference and manual for staff.

WORKING HEALTHY

QUIZ QUESTIONS & ANSWERS   E-1

MARK TRUE OR FALSE TO THE FOLLOWING QUESTIONS

1. It is okay to consume hot food items at warm temperatures because the food was initially heated at the correct temperature before service.
   True   False

2. Serving milk that was set at 60°F is okay if ice is added in the glass andto cool it down.
   True   False

3. If your hands look clean you do not need to wash them when returning to the kitchen after break.
   True   False

4. Having full trash bags on the floor is accepted because it is the night's staff job to toss out the trash and pest or rodents have not been seen today.
   True   False

5. It is okay to wipe my hands on my clothes after washing my hands because there were no paper towels in the bathroom.
   True   False

6. I know when to wash my hands; I can detect germs by looking at them.
   True   False

7. Germs, such as bacteria and viruses, grow easily so always think of your hands as contaminated.
   True   False

8. Germs are easy to see with your eyes.
   True   False

9. Food contamination may occur due to a food service worker whose hands were not washed right away.
   True   False

WORKING HEALTHY

QUIZ QUESTIONS & ANSWERS E-1

10. It is okay to wear the clothes I wore yesterday to work or a hat from my house instead of a hairnet; at least I came to work

 True   False

11. Potentially Hazardous Foods are foods that are more likely than others to grow germs that cause food poisoning.

 True   False

12. Hot foods are not potentially hazardous foods.

 True   False

13. Cold foods are not potentially hazardous foods.

 True   False

14. Cold foods are not potentially hazardous foods.

 True   False

15. When preparing cold items (potato salad, egg salad) you should start with cold ingredients.

 True   False

16. Wash your hands before handling salad ingredients.

 True   False

17. When preparing cold items (potato salad, egg salad) you should start with cold ingredients.

 True   False

18. Wash your hands before handling salad ingredients.

 True   False

19. When preparing cold items (potato salad, egg salad) you should start with cold ingredients.

 20. **True   False**

WORKING HEALTHY

QUIZ QUESTIONS & ANSWERS   E-1

21. Wash your hands before handling salad ingredients.

    True   False

21. Some pests that are known to infest food establishments include cockroaches, flies, weevils, mice and rats.

    True   False

21. We don't have to worry about cross contamination of ice; after all, ice is frozen and bacteria can't get into or grow in it.

    True   **False**

22. Check all the correct methods to keep pests out:

    ❏ Clean the entire department once a year.
    ❏ Clean the entire department monthly.
    ❏ Clean only my section of the department.
    ❏ ***Clean the department often and on a regular schedule***.
    ❏ Do not use screen doors as mice and rats can bit through the screen and enter the department.
    ❏ ***Use screen doors and cover small holes where mice and rats can get in.***
    ❏ Use garbage cans with ill-fitting lids
    ❏ ***Use garbage cans with fitted lids***
    ❏ ***Remove the garbage often***
    ❏ Remove the garbage once or twice a day. This eliminates the amount of time rats or mice could enter the premises.
    ❏ ***Keep the area around garbage containers clear of trash and litter.***
    ❏ ***Before using pesticides put away all food, and cover the work surfaces.***

WORKING HEALTHY

QUIZ QUESTIONS & ANSWERS   E-1

23. Check which of the following are correct sanitation and safety methods:

- ❏ Wash your hands when you see them full of germs.
- ❏ ***Wash you hands often and wash them wel,***
- ❏ Keep food in the "Danger Zone" for a few minutes after meal service.
- ❏ ***Prevent foodborne illness by keeping food out of the "Danger Zone," the temperatures in between 45°F and 145°F.***
- ❏ Prevent food poisoning by keeping food out of the "Danger Zone," the temperatures in between 70°F and 140°F.
- ❏ Cook food until they almost reach proper temperatures.
- ❏ ***Cook food until they reach proper temperatures.***
- ❏ ***Keep food safe from cross contamination with careful storage and sanitizing.***
- ❏ Store chemicals above or below food items
- ❏ ***Store chemicals for cleaning and pest control away from food, utensils and equipment.***
- ❏ Store chemicals for cleaning and pest control near food, utensils and equipment.
- ❏ Keep your workplace clean and safe by keeping cleaning and pest control near food
- ❏ Clean hoods when you see grease and dust accumulate on them
- ❏ ***Clean hoods every 2 weeks or more often if needed.***
- ❏ Wash filters quarterly.
- ❏ ***Wash filters weekly.***

WORKING SAFELY
QUIZ QUESTIONS & ANSWERS

E-2

IDENTIFY EACH STATEMENT AS SAFE OR UNSAFE   SAFE   UNSAFE

1. After dinner Sam mopped up the sauce he has spilled earlier.
Después de la cena Sam mapeó la salsa que había derramado anteriormente

2. Amy used a step ladder to reach the refrigerator top.
Amy se paró sobre una escalera para alanzar a limpiar encima de la nevera

3. Tom purchased a rug that had a non-skid back.
Tom compró una alfombra con goma que se pega por debajo

4. Sam used a dull knife to pare his apple.
Sam usó un cuchillo sin filo para partir su manzana

5. Anne didn't try to catch the falling knife in mid-air, but just let it drop to the floor.
Anne no trató de cojer el cuchillo que se le calló de las manos y lo dejó caer al piso

6. Andy put the steak knives in the dish water with the rest of the dishes.
Andy puso el cuchillo afilado en el agua de jabón con los demás platos

7. Ben poked a hole in the top of a can with a utility knife.
Ben hizo un boquete en la tapa de la lata con su cuchillo

8. Alex retrieved with his fingers as many pieces of the broken glass from the dishwater and floor as possible and wiped up the rest.
Alex sacó con sus dedos todos los pedazos de vidrio de la fregadora y el piso y luego le pasó paño al piso

9. Cathy cut the can lid completely off and threw it away inside the empty can.
Cathy cortó la tapa de la lata completamente y la botó adentro de la lata vacía

10. Dave lit a match first, then turned on the gas to his stove.
Dave prendió un fósforo primero y entonces abrió el gas en la estufa

11. Frank dropped the potato slices into the hot oil with his fingers.
Frank echo las lonjas de papas en el aceite caliente con sus dedos

WORKING SAFELY
QUIZ QUESTIONS & ANSWERS

E-2

IDENTIFY EACH STATEMENT AS SAFE OR UNSAFE   **SAFE   UNSAFE**

12. Harry smacked Jim on the back as he was leaning over to cough.
Harry le dio un puno a Jim por la espalda cuado se doblo a tozer porque se ahogo

13. Tom used a thick towel to take the cookies out of the oven.
Tom uso una tohalla gruesa para sacar las cookies del horno

14. Stacy used a wet pot holder to remove the boiling water from the stove.
Stacy uso un agarrador mojado para sacar la charola de agua hirviendo de la estufa

15. Karen turns the pan handles out when cooking because they are easier to reach.
Karen voltea el mango de las ollas hacia afuera cuando cocina pues asi las alcanza mejor

16. Earl used water to put the grease fire out.
Earl uso agua para apagar el fuego de grasa

17. Burt set the paper towels down next to the simmering soup on the stove.
Burt puso papeltohalla al lado de la sopa mientras la calentaba

18. Pete lifted the lid from the boiling water to peek into the pot and see if it was boiling already.
Pete levanto la tapa del agua hirviendo para ver si ya hervia

19. Amy wore her favorite 3 inch hoop earrings and 12 inch chain with a 2 inch cross to work today.
Amy se puso sus aretes favoritos de 3 pulbadas y su cadena de 12 pulgadas

Answers on next page

WORKING SAFELY
QUIZ QUESTIONS & ANSWERS   E-2

Answers to Working Safely Questions:
1. Unsafe
2. Safe
3. Safe
4. Unsafe
5. Safe
6. Unsafe
7. Unsafe
8. Unsafe
9. Safe
10. Unsafe
11. Safe
12. Unsafe
13. Unsafe
14. Unsafe
15. Un

COMPETENCE ASSESSMENT   E-3

This is an evaluation based on observations to determine competency in areas appropriate to a dining services staff sanitation and food safety responsibilities. It can be used by the direct supervisor, consultant, or as a self-assessment tool by the staff person after completing the Cleaning & Food Sanitation Guidelines book.

Place a check in the box to the right of each criterion and make comments as appropriate.

COMPETENCY	COMPLETED	ADDITIONAL TRAINING NEEDED
1. Knowledge and skill required to perform job duties: a. Is oberved handing and washing, pots, pans, measuring devices, and equipment following procedures. b. Demonstrates proper selection and use of utensils for portion- control & handles without cross-contamination. c. Demonstrates proper food handling in compliance with HACCP d. Verbalizes proper food cooking and holding temperatures. e. Verbalizes proper food storage procedures, temperatures & length of time f. Is able to read thermometers to measure temperature.		
2. Effective and safe use of all equipment used in job activities: a. Demonstrates safe and effective operation of equipment in the work area. b. Verbalizes proper procedures for reporting unsafe equipment.		
3. Safety and sanitation. a. Verbalizes understanding of proper use of chemicals, location and proper application. b. Verbalizes location of purpose of Material Safety Data Sheets **c.** (MSDS). d. Demonstrates proper procedures for cleaning equipment and work area. e. Demonstrates understanding of sanitation and safety standards. f. Demonstrates proper body mechanics to prevent injury.		
4. Prevention of contamination and transfer of infection: a. Verbalizes and demonstrates safe and sanitary practices for food handling and storage.		

Assessment Method: Demonstration, Observation or Self-assessment

EVALUATOR SIGNATURE:_____DATE:_____

STAFF SIGNATURE:_____DATE:_____

RESOURCES AND REFERENCES   F

1) *Applied Foodservice Sanitation.* The Educational Foundation of the National Restaurant Association. IL.

2) Axler, B., *Sanitation, Safety and Maintenance Management.* New York, NY: ITT Educational Services (1984).

3) *Bringing Food Safety to the Table.* Cooper Instrument Corporation. Middlefield, CT. (1996).

4) Cassens, D.I., *Simplified Diet and Nutrition Guidelines* (2017).

5) Cassens, D.I., *Orientation and Training Manual for Cooks* (2017).

6) Cassens, D.I., *Dining Services Orientation & Training* (2017).

7) Custer, M.J. *The Challenge of Contamination.* Chicago (1993).

8) County, State and Federal Regulations (you are responsible for reading and understanding those sections pertinent to your job, and ensuring that your department meets those standards).

9) *Eggs and Good Health.* Egg Nutrition Center. Washington, D.C.

10) FDA, HACCP, www.fda.gov/foodguidanceregulation/haccp

11) *Federal, State & County Retail Food Codes.* Most recent editions

12) *HACCP Reference Book.* 7th edition National Restaurant Association. Chicago.

13) *Infection Control in the Hospital.* Third Edition, Chicago, IL: American Hospital Association.

14) *Information for Consumers.* USDA, Food Safety and Inspection Service

RESOURCES AND REFERENCES F

15) King, H., *Food Safety Management: Implementing a Food Safety Program in a Food* National Restaurant Association, *ServSafe Manager 7th Ed.,USA.*

16) 16) Meyer, N., Managing Food Safety and Sanitation: A sanitation guide for the food service industry (2015).USDA, Food Safety and Inspection Service. *Information for Consumers.*

17) Shaw, I.C., Food Safety: *The Science of Keeping Food Safe.*(Dec 26, 2012).

18) State of California – Department of Health Services. *Foodservice Guide for Healthcare Facilities.* Sacramento, California

19) Greenfield, M.A., *48 Ways to Foil Food Infections.* Channing L. Bete Co., Inc.

20) *Sanitation of Food Service Establishments: A Guide for On-the-Job Training of Personnel.* Iowa State Department of Health Nutrition Service.

21) *ServSafe Coursebook.* 7th edition National Restaurant Association Education Foundation. USA.

22) *The Incredible Edible Egg.* American Egg Board.

23) *Training the Foodservice Worker.* Chicago, IL: Hospital Research and Education Trust (1974).

24) USDA Meat and Poultry Hotline: 1-800-535-4555.

25) *Sanitation of Food Service Establishments: A Guide for On-the-Job Training of Personnel.* Iowa State Department of Health Nutrition Service.

26) *ServSafe Coursebook.* U.S.A.: 5th edition National Education Foundation of the National Restaurant Association.

INDEX
Alphabetical order

PROCEDURE NUMER	TOPIC	PAGE
v	About Me	*v*
B	Cleaning and Sanitation Procedures	**12**
B18	Cleaning and Storage of Ice Scoop	**42**
B23	Cleaning of Ranges and Ovens	**47**
B24	Cleaning of Refrigerators and Freezers – Dietary	**48**
B28	Cleaning of Refrigerators in Nursing Units & Pantries	**54**
B25	Cleaning of Refrigerators in Resident Rooms	**50**
B27	Cleaning of Steamers and Steam Kettles	**53**
B3	Cleaning of Can Opener and Base	**15**
B7	Cleaning of Coffee Brewing Equipment	**20**
B2	Cleaning of Dining Areas	**14**
B6	Cleaning of Floors	**19**
B18	Cleaning of Ice Machines	**41**
C3	Cleaning Schedule Assignments & Procedures	**60**
C12	Cleaning Schedule Assignments & Procedure	**70**
D5	Common Causes of Foodborne Illness Food Safety Regulations	**96**
E	Competence	**103**
E4	Competence Assessment (Observation)	**111**
C8	Cooking and Cooling Log	**66**
ii	Copyrights & Credits	*ii*
C14	Daily Kitchen Cleaning Schedule	**74**
iv	Dedication	*iv*

INDEX
Alphabetical order

PROCEDURE NUMER	TOPIC	PAGE
vi	Deepak Chopra – Sanitation Quote	*vi*
C5	Deliveries Temperature Record	*63*
B12	Dispensing Equipment	*31*
B13	Dry Storage Areas	*33*
B14	Electrical Food Machines	*35*
A1	Employee Health and Personal Hygiene	*3*
A2	Empolyee Health and Safety	*4*
D1	Food From Outside Sources	*86*
D6	Food Safety Tips	*101*
D	Food Sanitation & Safety – Purpose	*85*
A3	Food Sanitation & Safety Guidelines	*5*
C2	Food Temperature Cooling Log	*59*
D6	Food Temperature Safety	*99*
B1	Food Thermometer Calibration	*13*
C	Forms Records and Logs	*55*
C6	Freezer Temperature Record	*64*
B9	General Dishroom Sanitation	*26*
B26	Green Buckets	*52*
D2	HACCP Management	*88*
C20	HACCP Plan Summary –ROP CCP HACCP	*81*
B21	Handling of Mops and Buckets	*45*
C19	Hazard Analysis Table – Process Step	*80*
B16	Hoods, Vents and Filters	*38*

INDEX
Alphabetical order

PROCEDURE NUMER	TOPIC	PAGE
B17	Hot Food Tables, Tray Carts, Shelves	39
B18	Ice Maker Manufacturer Instructions page	42
G	Index & Table of Contents - Alphabetical	114
B19	Ingredients Bins	43
B12	Juice Dispenser	31
B10	Machine Dishwashig, Drying and Storage	27
B11	Manual Dishwashing	29
B12	Milk Dispenser	31
D6	MinimuM Safe Internal Cooking Temperatures	100
B8	Monitoring Dishwashing Machines	22
C17	Monthly Kitchen Cleaning Schedule	77
B28	Patient Refrigerators Outside of Kitchen	54
B22	Pest Control and Monitoring	46
C23	Pest Control Monitoring Record	84
C9	Pots and Pans Sanitizer/Temperature Log	67
iii	Preface	iii
C13	Pre-Meal Checklist	73
B15	Prevention of Rodent Infestaton	37
C18	Production Schedules and Standards HACCP Based Instructions	78
C22	Quality Assessment of a Meal	83
C7	Refrigerator Temperature Record	65
F	Resources and References	112
D4	Safe Use of Gloves	93

INDEX
Alphabetical order

PROCEDURE NUMER	TOPIC	PAGE
A4	Safety and Accident Prevention Management	**9**
C1	Sanitation Review With comments	**56**
A	Sanitation Standards	**1**
B26	Sanitizing Cloths in Red Sanitizing Buckets	**51**
B5	Shelves, Contertops and Other Surfaces	**17**
C11	Storage Log – Refrigerator – Freezer	**69**
B20	Storage of Cleaning Supplies and Janitor's Closet	**44**
C21	Storage Time and Temperature Guidelines	**82**
vii	Table of Contents - Procedures and Sections	***vii***
D3	Temperature Guidelines	**92**
C4	Temperature Recods Cooking Temperature Record	**62**
C10	Thermometer Calibration Record	**68**
i	Title page	***I***
B4	Walls and Ceilings	**16**
C15	Weekly Kitchen Cleaning Schedule – Jan To June	**75**
C16	Weekly Kitchen Cleaning Schedule – June to Dec	**76**
E1	Working Healthy Quiz Questions and Answers	**104**
E2	Working Safely Quiz Questions and Answers	**108**

www.ingramcontent.com/pod-product-compliance
Lightning Source LLC
Chambersburg PA
CBHW080738230426
43665CB00020B/2782